WHAT DO
OTHER FAITHS
BELIEVE?

Marcus Borg -
Meeting Jesus again for the
first time

The End of Faith
Sam Harris (Both)

WHAT DO OTHER FAITHS BELIEVE?

A Study of World Religions

FaithQuestions SERIES

Paul Stroble

ABINGDON PRESS
NASHVILLE

WHAT DO OTHER FAITHS BELIEVE?
A Study of World Religions

By Paul Stroble

This book is printed on acid-free, elemental chlorine-free paper.

ISBN: 0-687-07550-5

05 06 07 08 09 10 11 12—10 9 8 7 6

MANUFACTURED IN THE UNITED STATES OF AMERICA

CONTENTS

ACKNOWLEDGMENTS

My thanks and deep appreciation go first to the interviewees for their time and their words. If someone approached you and asked you to discuss your religious beliefs *for publication,* how would you respond? Everyone helped me enormously and even took the time to read my resulting chapter drafts. I would also like to thank Dr. Arne Hassing and Dr. Tom Cleman of Northern Arizona University; Albert Plotkin, senior rabbi emeritus of Temple Beth Israel, Phoenix, Arizona; Dr. Jim Reinard of Greenville College; the late Dr. Carol Thysell of University of North Carolina-Wilmington; Ms. Amira Traish; Dr. David Odell-Scott of Kent State University; Dr. Rula Abisaab; Dr. Malek Abisaab; Rev. Dick Williams; Dow Chamberlain and Pamela Dilmore of The United Methodist Publishing House; and as always, Beth and Emily.

HOW TO USE
WHAT DO OTHER FAITHS BELIEVE?
A STUDY OF WORLD RELIGIONS

WHAT DO OTHER FAITHS BELIEVE? A STUDY OF WORLD RELIGIONS provides opportunities to learn about other religions and to compare beliefs with those of the Christian faith. The book is designed for use in any of three settings: (1) adult Sunday school, (2) weekday adult groups, and (3) retreat settings. It can also provide a meaningful resource for private study.

Sunday School: WHAT DO OTHER FAITHS BELIEVE? may be used on Sunday mornings as a short-term, seven-week study. Sunday morning groups generally last 45 to 60 minutes. If your group would like to go into greater depth, you can divide the chapters and do the study for longer than seven weeks.

Weekday Study: If you use WHAT DO OTHER FAITHS BELIEVE? in a weekday study, we recommend seven 90-minute sessions. Participants should prepare ahead by reading the content of the chapter and choosing one activity for deeper reflection and study. A group leader may wish to assign these activities. You may want to use the additional resources listed in "For More Information" at the end of Chapters 1–6.

Retreat Study: You may wish to use WHAT DO OTHER FAITHS BELIEVE? in a more intense study like a weekend retreat. Distribute the books at least two weeks in advance. Locate and provide additional media resources and reference materials, such as dictionaries of world religions, Bible dictionaries and commentaries, and sacred texts from other traditions if available. Tell participants to read WHAT DO OTHER FAITHS BELIEVE? before the retreat begins. Begin on Friday with an evening meal or refreshments followed by gathering time and worship taken from

"Gathering" in Chapter 1. Discuss Chapter 1. Cover Chapters 2, 3, 4, 5, and 6 on Saturday. Develop a schedule that includes time for breaks, for meals, and for personal reflection of various topics in the sessions. Cover Chapter 7 on Sunday. End the retreat with closing worship on Sunday afternoon.

Leader/Learner Helps

Leader/learner helps are located in boxes near the relevant main text. They include a variety of discussion and reflection activities. Include both the Gathering and Closing worship activities in each session, and choose from among the other leader/learner helps to fit the time frame you have chosen for your group.

The activities in the leader/learner helps meet the needs of a variety of personalities and ways of learning. They are designed to stimulate both solitary reflection and group discussion. An interactive and informal environment will encourage the interchange of ideas and demonstrate the value of diverse perspectives. While the readings may be done in the group, reading outside of the session will enrich individual reflection and group discussion.

Most of the chapters include a list of further research options in "For More Information." You will enrich your learning by reading one or more of the listed resources.

The Role of the Group Leader

A group leader facilitates gathering and closing worship, organizes the group for each session, monitors the use of time so that adequate attention is given to all major points of the session, and fosters an atmosphere of mutual respect and Christian caring. The leader should participate fully in the study as both learner and leader. The same person may lead all the sessions, or each session may have a different leader.

CHAPTER 1
UNDERSTANDING OTHER FAITHS

Why Study World Religions?

Focus: This chapter looks at different perspectives in approaching world religions and shows the value of appreciating other religions.

Imagine a group of church people discussing world religions. The people's comments represent a variety of approaches and attitudes about other faiths.

"No religion except Christianity is true!" says Ted. "I stand on Acts 4:12. That's why we have preachers and evangelists. People are perishing because of their false religions."

"Religions all teach basically the same thing," says Becky, "the Golden Rule, selflessness, truthfulness, the unimportance of wealth and success, the importance of love and service, the importance of

Gathering

Introduce yourselves. Do an "ice breaking" game. Write names of religious leaders—Gandhi, Buddha, Dr. Martin Luther King, Jr., Mother Teresa, the Dalai Lama, and others—on index cards and tape one card on each group member's back. Be sure not to let the person see the card on his or her back. Let each participant try to guess the name of the person by asking other group members questions about the person.

Make a list of questions you would like to explore in these sessions. Tell the group about your list. Pray for God's guidance and support as you explore these questions and others during the study.

Read the discussion among people at church. Which point of view coincides most closely with yours? Which is most different from yours? What do you know about world religions? Which religions do you think you understand the best? the most poorly? What have been your experiences with religions other than your own? Do you think other religions are (1) scary, (2) a source of wisdom, (3) a way to be misled, or (4) merely interesting?

'true' as opposed to 'rote' worship, and so on. Even though I've staked my claim on one religion, I don't see how you can say the rest of them are false."

"There's a certain amount of—I hate to call it 'political correctness,' " notes Anisa, "but whenever religiously motivated violence happens in the world, someone rushes to defend religions as 'really' about love. There's plenty of hatred and violence in Christianity, too—now and historically. Concerning religions, I get confused about what they 'really' believe and what I hear in the media."

Rodney interjects, "Honestly, I've been in and out of church over the years—mostly in. But if I don't feel like I'm being fed, I just do some searching on my own. I agree with Becky. In fact, the things I read about other religions help me understand Christianity better."

"I had to read Huston Smith's *The Religions of Man* in college," says Bob, "but like most of the rest of my college courses I can't remember what I read. And I accidentally taped the Super Bowl over my PBS Joseph Campbell episodes. Sorry."

Why study world religions? Let's think through this imaginary conversation, to orient us as we look at several world faiths together.

"No Religion But Christianity Is True"

To some people, studying other faiths is like consulting the instruction book for an outmoded tool they do not plan to use. Their own faith is the true one, the reliable interpretation of God and reality. Therefore, studying different beliefs is unnecessary—maybe even risky. Some Christians would consider world religions as paths away from the truth of Christ. Dr. Diana L. Eck of Harvard University puts the matter well. "In thinking about other faiths, most churchgoing Christians have imprinted upon their minds a few lone fragments of scripture. There is John 14:6. . . . There is Acts 4:12. . . . This is all the theological equipment they have to grapple with a new world of many faiths."[1] One could consider John 3:16-18

("For God so loved the world that he gave his only Son, so that everyone who believes in him may not perish but may have eternal life. Indeed, God did not send the Son into the

Find a copy at your nearby book store, or on your favorite Internet book site, of Diana L. Eck's *Encountering God: A Spiritual Journey from Bozeman to Banares* (Boston: Beacon Press, 1993), and her *A New Religious America: How a "Christian Country" Has Become the World's Most Religiously Diverse Nation* (San Francisco: HarperSanFrancisco, 2001). What are some of Dr. Eck's conclusions about different faiths?

world to condemn the world, but in order that the world might be saved through him. Those who believe in him are not condemned; but those who do not believe are condemned already, because they have not believed in the name of the only Son of God") alongside John 14:6b ("No one comes to the Father except through me") and Acts 4:12 ("There is salvation in no one else, for there is no other name under heaven . . . by which we must be saved").

Religious belief demands both commitment and wholehearted allegiance, so investigating other faiths seems a detour off the straight path.

Other passages of Scripture, however, are different from the views above. Matthew 7:1-6 admonishes us not to judge others lest we be judged. Matthew 7:21-23 says that professing Jesus is not the password that gets you to heaven. Matthew 25:31-46 says, "all the nations," including those who did not know the Lord of Israel, are judged by their acts of mercy alone. In Romans 11:22, Paul strictly warns that God's kindness to Gentile

Look up these verses in the Bible: Matthew 25:31-46; John 8:12; 10:16; 14:6; Romans 3:9; and Ephesians 3:5-6. How do you think these passages apply to our study? Look up the word *gods* in a Bible concordance. What is the Old Testament attitude toward other religious outlooks? How do you think the Old Testament view may or may not apply today?

List ways that you think religions provide evidence of their truth. What evidence would you offer for the truth of your own faith?

Do you know anyone who is particularly "doctrinaire" in his or her religious belief? What is this person's basis for certainty? Do you feel strengthened or put-off by people who seem particularly "sure of themselves" religiously?

[handwritten margin notes: p 32; sheep + goats; p 117; p 122; p 171; Did not accept other gods.]

Christians should make one humble and careful rather than arrogant, for that kindness can be lost. In other words, the Scriptures are rich concerning God's mercy toward human beings and should be considered together. "A few lone fragments of scripture" do not give us permission to be religiously smug—strong though our convictions may be.

Religions Teach the Same Basic Truths

Without a doubt, there are very strong similarities among faiths in both form and content. The late Joseph Campbell popularized similarities and common themes among religions through his books and his 1980s PBS series with Bill Moyers. Many religions teach that there is a basic problem with human beings. We are spiritually "damaged"; we need help outside ourselves to overcome this fault. God—or the divine principle—is favorably disposed to this problem and is willing to help us. In some faiths—Christianity and Hinduism, though unequivocally not Islam and Judaism—God has taken form on earth. Most religions have kinds of heavenly angels, messengers, or saints who can also guide and protect persons.

Many religions have stories of persons who must undergo times of solitude, journeying, and/or testing. The stories of Moses, Jesus, Muhammad, Siddhartha, and others contain such episodes. Many religions have stories of persons who experience an extraordinary divine call—Abraham, Moses, the Hebrew prophets, Muhammad, Nanak, the Bab, Baha'u'llah, and others. By faith, we choose which witnesses to believe.

Nearly all religions have a version of "the Golden Rule"; indeed, it was taught hundreds of years before Jesus. Many religions emphasize truthfulness, peacemaking, wisdom over wealth, forgiveness, respect for parents and the elderly, service to the needy. Many teach that service to others is more important than serving the self. In fact service to others is often seen as religious devotion and as being more important than the procedures of formal worship. Many teach the primacy of love and unity, and the evils of hatred and revenge.[2]

The commonalities among religions are quite striking and are sufficient to make thoughtful persons respect rather than disdain other faiths. It is simplistic to say that all religions but one are wholly false.

At the same time, to stress commonalities without noting significant divergences pays no respect to the religions that we study. Many essential beliefs among religions cannot be reconciled at the very basic levels, in their particular expressions of belief. For instance, the primacy of Jesus as the source of salvation is not an idea shared by other faiths. The divine authority of the particular Scriptures like the Bible, the Qur'an, the *Vedas,* or the *Adi Granth* are not universally acknowledged by the different faiths; nor is the special witness of the Hebrew people, and so on. Even common beliefs often cannot be properly separated from the particular religious context in which they occur. For instance, Jesus' teaching of the Golden Rule is not a general moral principle but an interpretation of the Torah in light of his own messianic ministry. If one follows the core teachings of all religions, one will undoubtedly become a "spiritual," moral person, yet will miss important truths, blessings, and mysteries peculiar to specific faiths—as if you appreciated the laws of a nation but rejected the duties of citizenship.

Some religions incorporate diversity better than others. According to some religions, persons will receive spiritual benefit whether or not they follow that particular religion. Christians insist on belief in Jesus, but Hindus will not insist that Christians or anyone else should believe in Vishnu. Hindus will not even insist that other Hindus should believe in

---

Spiritual Types

Many Christians don't realize that everyone has his or her own spiritual type. In other words, we learn faith and grow spiritually in different ways. A book that explains this well is Corinne Ware's *Discover Your Spiritual Type: A Guide to Individual and Congregational Growth* (Washington, DC: The Alban Institute, 1995). Ware discusses four broadly defined spiritual types[3]:

- "Head" Spirituality. This person thinks through religious ideas and appreciates good sermons, good books, writing, and other activities involving logical thought.
- "Heart" Spirituality. This person experiences spiritual reality in a more emotional way: through such activities as music, testimony, and spontaneous rather than liturgical services.
- "Mystic" Spirituality. This person experiences spiritual reality in nonverbal, contemplative ways: through meditation, intuitive insight into God's reality, or a simple lifestyle.
- "Kingdom" Spirituality. Such a person finds spirituality in action, work, social justice, and striving for a vision.

What type are you? How does your spiritual type reflect your understanding of other religions?

Vishnu! Many Buddhists dispense with theistic belief altogether and choose instead to focus upon spiritual practices. Jews do not believe you must keep all the laws of the Torah in order to be redeemed, and Jews certainly do not insist that Gentiles should be members of a synagogue. The doctrines and practices of other faiths are suitable for different cultures and peoples and need not be the only way to God. To claim otherwise is, in a way, disrespectful to God—as if God would not provide ways by which many, many people might come to God.

Other religions are not as accepting of diversity. God has provided clear ways by which people might know God, and that way is found in the sacred texts like the Qur'an or the Bible. People just need to find out about those ways. If they do not, we should pray for God's gracious love rather than judgment.

Understanding the "Real" Religion

Even a beginning knowledge of world faiths helps one understand many aspects of our modern world. Religion is a key element in human societies throughout history. Although our own era is deeply indebted to Enlightenment separations of church and state and of religion and science, religious belief has by no means declined in the wake of secularism and modernity, contrary to the predictions of philosophers and social scientists not so long ago. In fact, religious belief has been growing as well as diversifying throughout the world; the daily news is filled with stories, sadly, many negative ones, in which religion figures prominently. The United States has become, in Diana Eck's words, "the most religiously diverse nation on earth."[4] And although some people consider "diversity" a liberal mantra that waters down meaning, the fact remains: one need not look far to find people of different religious faith. Accepting diversity means living in a society in which not everyone is the same.

Read about *modernity* and *secularism* in the box on page 15 and in a dictionary or encyclopedia that defines these terms. How does our culture show secular traits? scientific traits? religious traits? In your opinion, which terms best describe our culture?

Because religious belief has become so pervasive and diverse, understanding world faiths helps one to be truthful and knowledgeable. We pick up religious stereotypes unintentionally. Many Christians, for instance, have a very poor understanding of Judaism. Seldom do

John's gospel

the Christian Scriptures mention "the Jews" except in a negative way, even though the New Testament was mostly written by Jews. The Scriptures give an unsympathetic glimpse of a time of conflict between two different Jewish groups, that is, "mainstream" Jewish leaders and the first generation of Christians, rather than a broader view of Judaism as a whole.

Similarly, in news of world events in which religion plays some part,

The dictionary defines *secularism* as a rejection of or indifference to religious beliefs. *Modernity,* which is related to secularism, is a term referring to several aspects of our contemporary era, including industrial and technological economies, the freedom of scientific inquiry (in which truth is seen as empirical and verifiable), and governments that guarantee the freedom and autonomy of the individual who, in turn, has a voice in government. Some people see these things as strengthening religion by giving people freedom for a broad range of religious expression. Others see secularism and modernity as a threat, for instance, those who oppose the teaching of evolution (at the expense of creationism and intelligent design) in public schools, or those who oppose the legality of abortion.

the media seldom provide a full and complete view of the religion in question. The result is that many of us have stereotyped views of different faiths. For instance, I well remember carrying very superficial views of Islam, drawn primarily from mid-1980s reports of Middle Eastern civil wars and kidnappings of Western journalists. One similarly picks up negative portrayals of Sikhs, Hindus, Christians, Jews, and others from news reports from world hot spots.

As Charles Kuralt wrote in another context, "The front pages were full of selfishness, arrogance and hostility toward others. The back roads were another country."[5] Understanding world faith puts us on a kind of back-roads journey toward respect and appreciation.

The Wisdom of Other Faiths Enriches One's Own

It is tempting to minimize the spiritual experiences of other people. By doing so, I thereby assume my own experience is the best or only one! A better way is to recognize that each of us learns in different ways and each of us brings our particular experiences to our religious journeys. This is not relativism or subjectivism; this is simply the breadth and depth of human understanding. Dr. Rob Schwartz of the University of Akron told me about Buddhism:

> If someone is very connected with a certain religion, or very involved with it, there's something intrinsic about the person themselves that draw them to that particular philosophy. The core of most religions is very much the same, with similar principles. The "guiding light" is very similar. But the outside part, the "dressing," is very different sometimes. The different ways that religions portray themselves to people attract certain kinds of personalities. The person that I am and aspire to be—patient, calm, compassionate, tolerant, accepting—drew me to Buddhism because those are some of the core principles. I've always been interested in Asia and Asian culture, and Buddhism is very much a part of that culture. Because of my interest in Asia, I began to read books about Buddhism. I realized very, very quickly that the core life values are things that I believe strongly, but they're principles that could help people feel more happy and more fulfilled. I grew up in a Jewish family; most of my family is still Jewish. That had a lot of benefits, but I felt like something was lacking there. Something didn't quite touch my heart or help me completely develop as a person. Buddhism has really helped me fill in that gap. That's why I got interested and started reading more about it.

In a recent speech, former president Jimmy Carter spoke of the other side of the coin. Religious extremism, or a fundamentalism that leads to violence, comes from "one's own personal relationship with God," he noted. "The first step is to feel that our faith is superior. . . . The second step is to believe that anyone who disagrees with us is also disagreeing with God." The third step, he said, "is to say that those who disagree with God are . . . not only mistaken, but inferior"; and finally the fourth step is "to say that those who disagree with God, their lives are not worthy in the eyes of God. . . . When religious faith is distorted to elevate, not God . . . but to exalt ourselves as the singular and chosen believers, that's when the cruelty comes and the basic principles of our faith are abandoned."[6]

> Read Philippians 3:4-11. What has Paul counted as loss? What has he gained?
>
> At this stage of your study, what religious beliefs seem to you to be common to several faiths? Do you know anyone who has converted to religious faith from another religion? Do you know anyone who has converted to religion from atheism or agnosticism? What happened to the person? What was his or her story?

Religions, especially "Western" religions, demand one's allegiance. For instance, in Philippians 3:4-11, Paul considers his Jewish heritage as "refuse" in order to gain Christ. And yet Paul did not give up his heritage, only its "perks." Paul's theological ideas—Messiah, atonement, justification, sacrifice, glorifying God through one's life, the Resurrection and Final Judgment—

> Have you ever known anyone who enjoyed "sampling" ideas from different religions and philosophies? Have you ever "picked and chosen" from among religious ideas? What do you see as the pitfalls and benefits?

are all Jewish ideas deeply held by Paul the converted Christian.

Sometimes doctrines from another faith can enrich one's own theological understanding. This does not mean that one is about to adopt a different faith! But a doctrine from another religion, a particular emphasis, can put a different "spin" on something you believe. Once, when I was feeling anxious, I was struck by the Muslim notion of *shirk*. The word means "idolatry," but it can also mean putting something ahead of God, or attributing to something or someone more power than God has. You can be guilty of idolatry if you are simply afraid; isn't God greater than that person or thing that you dread? Such an idea puts one's anxiety in perspective. Like Rob Schwartz, I have felt attracted to certain Buddhist doctrines. For me, the idea of "nonattachment" has been very helpful, especially when I'm stuck in some situation that makes me unhappy. One of the purposes of this book is to help readers gain clarity and insight for their own Christian faith-journeys by drawing from the wellsprings of other traditions.

Approaching World Religions

I came to world religions as an obligation and continued the study out of love for the subject. During my first undergraduate semester, I read Huston Smith's classic book *The Religions of Man* for a "Christianity and Culture" course taught by Dr. Jim Reinhard at Greenville College.[7] Like my imaginary churchgoer, I forgot what I'd read—but I kept the book. Twelve years later, new to the humanities department at Northern Arizona University, I was assigned to teach an introductory world religions course. Although I felt that I had a strong knowledge of Judaism and Christianity, my course work on world religions amounted to little except that Huston Smith book. I began with that text and started to work. As the saying goes, the best way to learn a subject is to teach it. I kept at least one class period ahead of my students. If anyone asked a question to which I knew no answer, I simply promised to look it up and report back. As I prepared my lectures on Islam, I remember my horror in discovering how much of my knowledge of Islam was based upon stereotypes and news reports. I kept working and found my way into other Eastern religions, about which I knew even less than I knew about Islam. Eventually I taught that course several times at Northern Arizona University and at other universities.

The following chapters include both my own words and the words of others. Working with each faith, I kept in mind particular questions. Rather than describe other religions as an outsider, I wanted believers within each faith tradition to describe their faith. I sought out people and interviewed them concerning their faith: what was their "take" on their own religion. I avoided the religious "professionals" and instead sought people who, while working in other jobs and fields besides religion, considered religious belief very important. I gave each person the following questions in advance and allowed each to respond as he or she desired.

- What is the nature of God/divinity?
- What is sin?
- What is forgiveness and on what basis is it conferred?
- What are the elements of worship?
- What are the ethical demands?
- What is the future beyond death?
- What is the view of other faiths?
- What are the scriptures?
- What are a few, quick historical highlights?

The interviews did not adhere slavishly to these questions—some aren't so apropos in describing Eastern ideas—but the questions formed the departure-point for discussion.

I deliberately sought people who lived in, or who were in some way connected to, my own geographical area, which is northeastern Ohio. My reason was not personal convenience. Rather I wanted to make an "object lesson": persons of different faiths are, literally as well as figuratively, our neighbors. I let my interviewees read my chapters in final draft so they would know I used their words properly and that my own "take" on each religion was fair and accurate. Several interviewees made corrections or clarifications to my text. Any remaining errors are my own.

One might object that people's individual "takes" on their religion is not representative of that religion. This is certainly true, but that is a risk of any presentation of a thing as vital and controversial as religion. Many Christians, I have found, are surprisingly uneasy about grappling with religious questions—as if the truth must always be perfectly clear—while even very conservative Jews and Muslims, for instance, assume that the truth will have to be interpreted, argued about, grappled with, and journeyed after. The pages of this study book represent the "grapplings" of several people—including myself—and invite you to join the journey.

> **Closing**
> Pray together Romans 11:33, 36. "O the depth of the riches and wisdom and knowledge of God! How unsearchable are his judgments and how inscrutable his ways! . . . For from him and through him and to him are all things. To him be the glory forever. Amen."

Notes

1. Diana L. Eck, *Encountering God: From Bozeman to Banares* (Boston: Beacon Press, 1993), page 16.

2. Jeffrey Moses, *Oneness: Great Principles Shared by All Religions*. New York: Fawcett Columbine, 1989.

3. Corinne Ware, *Discover Your Spiritual Type: A Guide to Individual and Congregational Growth* (Washington, DC: The Alban Institute, 1995), pages 28–45.

4. Diana L. Eck, *A New Religious America: How a "Christian Country" Has Become the World's Most Religiously Diverse Nation* (San Francisco: HarperSanFrancisco, 2001), page 4.

5. Quoted in Brad Herzog, *States of Mind: A Search for Faith, Hope, Inspiration, Harmony, Unity, Friendship, Love, Pride, Wisdom, Honor, Comfort, Joy, Bliss, Freedom, Justice, Glory, Triumph, and Truth or Consequences in America* (Winston-Salem: John F. Blair Publisher, 1999), page 5.

6. Quoted in *EthicsDaily.com* E-newsletter (Baptist Center for Ethics), December 4, 2002.

7. Originally published 1958. Revised and updated edition. *The World's Religions,* San Francisco: HarperSanFrancisco, 1992.

For More Information

Look for books and textbooks that discuss world religions:

• T. Patrick Burke, *The Major Religions: An Introduction with Texts.* Cambridge, MA: Blackwell Publishers, 1996.
• James C. Livingston, *Anatomy of the Sacred: An Introduction to Religion.* Third edition. Upper Saddle River, NJ: Prentice Hall, 1998.
• Michael Molloy, *Experiencing the World's Religions: Tradition, Challenge, and Change.* Second edition. Mountain View, CA: Mayfield, 2002.
• Lucinda Joy Peach, *Women and World Religions.* Upper Saddle River, NJ: Prentice Hall, 2002.
• Ninian Smart, *Worldviews: Crosscultural Explorations of Human Beliefs.* Third edition. Upper Saddle River, NJ: Prentice Hall, 2000.
• Huston Smith, *The World's Religions: Our Great Wisdom Traditions.* Revised edition of *The Religions of Man.* San Francisco: HarperSanFrancisco, 1992.

CHAPTER 2
THE LORD IS ONE

Judaism

One of the memorable experiences of my childhood was a visit to a synagogue. I grew up in Vandalia, a small,

Focus: In this session we examine Judaism, its history and basic beliefs.

southern Illinois town. During a two-week vacation Bible school at the local Methodist church—coincidentally, the Six-Day War was also happening—we took a field trip to the nearest temple, located in a town thirty miles south. I loved the Hebrew calligraphy and the large Torah scrolls. The field trip provided a very positive and formative first experience with Judaism. Years later, when I read the story of the Gentile centurion who sent Jewish elders to ask Jesus to heal his slave (Luke 7:1-10), I understood that story's expression of the Jewish-Gentile good will. *p 72*

Judaism has about 18 million adherents in the world—a small number among the great world religions—yet, Judaism has had a profound effect upon the history of the Western world. The oneness of God, the fact that God is revealed through ethical standards, the fact that God acts in human history, the emphasis upon worshiping God not only through religious rites but especially through serving others—

Gathering

If you are studying this chapter in a group, introduce yourselves. If you did not do so during the first session, take a moment to tell interesting things about yourself to one another. Ask for support and prayers, for yourself or other people. Pray for these concerns and for God's presence and prompting during the session.

> Brainstorm all the things that come to your mind when you think of *Jews* and *Judaism*. Some might think of *Fiddler on the Roof*. Others might think of people like Stephen Spielberg, Louis Brandeis, Albert Einstein, and others. What about Judaism do you not understand? Form groups of two or three and work together to pool your common knowledge of this faith.

all these are Jewish ideas bequeathed to Christianity, Islam, and to world religion generally. When you read the Sermon on the Mount, you are reading deeply Jewish teachings. Paul's major ideas about the Messiah, the Atonement, and the justification of sinners, and his style of interpreting Scripture are "reconfigured" Jewish ideas. Both Christianity and Islam stand in ambivalent relation to Judaism. Both religions affirm basic truths of Judaism but claim that God has spoken in additional ways. Judaism, meanwhile, has been called both particular and universal; in other words, its teachings concern the Jewish people in particular, but God also blesses persons of all ethnic and religious backgrounds.

> ### Yiddish
> Do you ever use words like *kvetch, chutzpah, schlep, klutz, mishmash, nebbish, shtik,* or *maven*? You're using the Yiddish language! Yiddish, which comes from the similarly pronounced German word for "Jewish" (*Jüdisch*), is a Jewish dialect incorporating medieval German and other languages. A historically significant language that has helped bond Jews together for centuries, many Yiddish expressions like these and others have entered English usage. If you do not know these words, look them up in most any English dictionary.

Greta Foster, endowment director of the Jewish Community Board of Akron, and Alvin Salzman, a Holocaust survivor who is former general manager of the West Point Market in Akron, Ohio, sat with me over coffee at the Market one day and explained several aspects of Jewish beliefs and practices. On another occasion, Dr. Stan Silverman, professor of social science at the University of Akron, invited me into his office and reflected on my several questions.

Historical Highlights

Ms. Foster pointed me to Genesis 14:13, where the word *Hebrew* is first mentioned in reference to Abraham's tribe and divine call. The ancient terms *Hebrew* and *Israelites* name those Middle Eastern tribes that entered the land of Canaan (Palestine) during the second millennium B.C. In the Genesis sto-

22

ries familiar to many, Abraham migrated with his family to Canaan around 2000 B.C. and his descendents populated the area. Hebrews eventually settled in Egypt and became slaves there. The Hebrew leader Moses and his family led the people from Egypt back to Canaan around the 1200s B.C.

By the 1000s B.C., the monarch David had established a United Kingdom thus creating a sense of national identity.

> **Vocabulary in the Hebrew Bible**
> • Israel: "One who contends with God," the name given to Jacob when he wrestled the mysterious angel at Peniel (Genesis 32:22-32). "Israelites" are biblical-era descendants of Jacob.
> • Canaan: the grandson of Noah. Noah cursed Canaan and his descendants, the Canaanites, thus explaining the enmity between Israelites and Canaanites (Deuteronomy 7:1-2). Canaan is also another name for the land of the Canaanites, which the Israelites settled.
> • Palestine: Another name for the land claimed by the Israelites. The name comes from "Philistine," one of the several peoples who lived in the land during biblical times. Find a Bible dictionary or concordance and study how the terms *Israel, Canaan, Palestine, land of milk and honey*, and *land* are used in the Scriptures.

Eventually the United Kingdom separated into two nations and each was eventually conquered. Assyria conquered the Northern Kingdom of Israel in 722 B.C., and the Babylonians conquered the Southern Kingdom of Judah in 586 B.C. Strictly speaking, Judaism as we know it emerged in the late 500s B.C. and following, when the Hebrews—now called Jews after their kingdom, Judah—returned to Canaan, reorganized religious life under the reforms of Ezra and Nehemiah, and reconstructed the Temple. Some of the features of the renewed faith included the observation of holidays, "kosher" laws, rabbis, and synagogues.

Jewish rabbis—the word *rabbi* means "teacher"—developed traditions of biblical interpretation that were eventually written in the multi-volume Talmud. After the Romans destroyed Jerusalem and the Temple in A.D. 70, Jews were scattered throughout the Middle Eastern and European worlds. They retained their culture through close study of the Scriptures and preservation of the Talmudic traditions. Never a majority in any country, Jews survived in Islamic and Christian kingdoms. The Kabbalah, a strong tradition of Jewish mysticism, developed in Europe during the late medieval era.

Jews were often persecuted, however, and forced to convert to

Christianity. They were falsely accused of crimes. Many people blamed Jews for the Black Death in the 1300s. Jews were often expelled from the countries in which they lived. Spain drove them out in 1492. Eastern European Jews included descendants of Jews expelled during earlier centuries from England and Germany.

The Nazi extermination of 6 million Jews was unique among Jewish persecutions for its technological efficiency and for the horrors inflicted on Jews, as well as the pervasive indifference, both in Europe and abroad, to the genocide. For the first time since the Roman conquest, Jews reestablished a homeland in Palestine and declared the independence of Israel in 1948.

Scriptures

Jewish Scripture is called the *Tanak* (sometimes spelled *Tanakh*) or simply the Hebrew Bible. Christians call this material the Old Testament. It is essentially the same material, but it is arranged in a different order partly because

---

Archaeological Discoveries and Scriptures

In 2001, *U.S. News and World Report* published an issue called *Mysteries of Faith* that discusses archaeological evidence and biblical narrative. See if your local library has a copy on file.

Many archaeological discoveries tend to support biblical stories. The first historical reference to David, outside the Bible, was discovered on a monument in northern Israel in 1993, for instance. But while the Book of Joshua tells of a military invasion and destroyed cities, archaeologists do not find evidence of such a conquest. See also Jeffery L. Sheler, *Is the Bible True? How Modern Debate and Discoveries Affirm the Essence of the Scripture* (HarperSanFrancisco, 1999). Study some of these discoveries.

In some ways, archaeological discoveries make no difference. Mr. Salzman told me, "We [Jews] didn't make Moses for a god. We buried him, and no one knows where his grave is so that it shall not become a shrine [Deuteronomy 34:5-6]. If someone found this grave today it would make no difference to the religion because he was not a god. He was inspired by God."

What is your view of the value of archaeological discoveries and what they can teach us about the Scriptures? What challenges you about such discoveries? What makes you want to know more? Do you agree or disagree with Mr. Salzman? Why or why not?

In "John" flowed Jews but now modified in translation.

early Christians read Greek versions like the Septuagint, a translation from Alexandria, Egypt. The Word *Tanak* is an acrostic of the three words *Torah, Nevi'im* and *Ketu'vim*. These words represent three different types of material that, in English, are also called Instruction, Prophets, and Writings.

For Jews the Torah, the name for the first five books, is the most important part of the Bible. The Torah begins with the creation of the world and tells the story of humankind and its decline into sin. It recounts the history of God's people from the call of Abraham through the death of Moses—about 2500 years of history if one takes literally the creation accounts and the genealogies.

The highlights of the Torah are God's covenant and God's law. The covenant (*brith*) is the agreement between God and God's people. God will bless and provide for the people and requires their faithfulness. Yet God's love does not stop when people sin. The Torah laws include the well-known Ten Commandments and many other commandments traditionally numbered at 613. Some of the laws are no longer applicable, such as the specifications for the Tabernacle and the laws governing sacrifice. Other laws dealt with civil cases that would have arisen when the Israelites were an independent society. Some laws, such as the dietary laws, are still observed by many Jews. "I don't believe the texts written 3,000 years ago are 100 percent applicable," says Mr. Salzman, who is a member of a conservative synagogue. "Now, the bases and foundations [of those texts]: those you have to believe."

Why is the law important? It defines what is God's will for us, but it also trains us. Since Jews believe in free will but not original sin, the law provides God's ethical standards. "Sin is [defined as] going against the commandments," says Prof. Silverman, "but also going against the 'subcategories' of commandments, if you will—caring for others, worshiping, justice, and so on."

Several Ways of Keeping the Torah

Just as Christianity has many denominations, Judaism has several branches. *Orthodox* is the most conservative branch of Judaism, keeping the commandments very literally, yet also struggling to understand them and to be obedient to them. In Orthodox worship, men and women do not sit together in worship. Orthodox Jewish

Do you consider yourself a liberal or conservative interpreter of Scripture? What biblical teachings challenge you? How do you think a reader can discern the difference between the eternal truths in some Scriptures and the teachings that reflect first-century culture?

> Visit a synagogue. Call to find times for the Shabbat (sabbath) services on Friday evening and Saturday morning. When you call, ask which service might be best to attend; you'll be welcomed, but you might feel more comfortable knowing what to expect. What parts of the service seemed more familiar? less familiar?

men will sometimes grow their beards and side hair in literal obedience to Scripture (Leviticus 19:27). *Conservative* Jews are more "moderate" in their observance and in their scriptural interpretation. Many keep the dietary laws, but do not consider all the Torah laws applicable for today. In Conservative and Orthodox worship, men wear a *kipa* (plural *kipot,* also called a *yarmulke*), a small head covering signifying humility to God. In *Reformed* worship, kipot are dispensed with and the Torah teachings are observed, especially in light of social justice needs, in the tradition of the Hebrew prophets. As Prof. Silverman points out, "There are songs, but not instrumental music in Conservative, but both in Reform. The mix of Hebrew to English is more toward Hebrew in Conservative than in Reform." Similarly Orthodox worship stresses Hebrew and has no instrumental music.

Contrary to views of many conservative Christians, Jews do not believe you have to keep perfectly all Torah laws in order to be spiritually blessed. Likewise, Jews believe that righteous Gentiles, who do not have to follow the Torah laws, will have a share in "the world to come."

Interpreting Scripture is a process of discovering truth more than rote obedience to the letter. Both Jews and Christians study the Scriptures in order to learn God's will. Many Christians are perplexed that Jews do not consider the New Testament scriptural; part of the reason has to do with Christian theology about Jesus.

The Messiah

> Read Isaiah 52 and 53. Why do you think Christians find these Scriptures helpful as they try to understand Jesus? How would they be helpful to Jewish people who heard these words centuries before Jesus was born?

Although Christians claim Jesus as the Jewish Messiah, most Jews disagree, although many will acknowledge that Jesus' teachings are deeply indebted to ancient Hebrew teachings. They point out that the Messiah is supposed to bring a reign of peace and redemption, both for Jews and non-

Jews, and Jews do not see this happening with the life of Jesus. Furthermore, Christians have often hated and persecuted Jews, often because of the New Testament's hostile attitude toward Jews, undercutting the claim that Jesus is the promised king of peace. Similarly, Christians combine two ideas, Messiah

> Pretend that you are a Jew coming to Christianity for the first time. What about Christianity would seem familiar, objectionable, or strange?

and Atonement, in a way foreign to messianic theology. In other words, the Messiah is supposed to be a bringer of peace, not a sacrifice for sin. Scriptural passages such as Isaiah 52–53 probably refer to the Jewish people as a whole rather than the particular Jew Jesus.

Nature of God

I asked about Jewish belief in God. "As I was taught when growing up," says Prof. Silverman, "God is not 'a being.' There is only one God, and he's everywhere. There is no shape or form to God. God expects us to glorify him through our actions."

"The nature of God] has been debated for generations," said Mr. Salzman. "God created man in his own image and made man a little less than the angels. Then the great philosopher Maimonides said, he doesn't have a body or a soul. He is a spirit." Maimonides, who lived in the twelfth century, noted that we cannot know God as God is, but rather as God acts.

YHWH is the name God revealed to Moses. It is rendered in English as "the Lord." Hebrew originally had no vowels; and the original pronunciation (Probably *Yahweh*) has been lost, since in order to show respect for God, God's name was not to be spoken. When Scripture is read in synagogues, the word *Adonai* ("Master" or "Lord") is substituted in the reading. Eventually Hebrew developed a system of vowel "points" that were placed beneath the Hebrew consonants. The vowel points of "Adonai" were added to the word *YHWH* ostensibly to remind people reading Scripture to say, "Adonai." When the Old Testament was rendered into English, translators mistakenly combined the two names to get *Yahowaih*, or more euphoniously, *Jehovah*.

The name YHWH is related to God's name "I am that I am" (*ehyeh asher ehyeh*) revealed to Moses. God is also named *Elohim* (God), *El Shaddai* ("God almighty" or "God of the mountain").

The history of the covenant people proves God's existence through the way God is seen to act in that history. God exists when the outnumbered people emerge victorious. Jews believe they are God's "chosen people," not because they are better than other people but because they bear witness to God's existence. God has created the universe. But the universe is so full and complex that we cannot begin to fathom all its aspects nor all the ways of its Creator. Thus Job, trapped in his own horrible suffering, found solace in the realization that God's ways are vast and incomprehensible.

Witnessing to God

God is never portrayed artistically in Judaism because God is Spirit rather than body. Enter a typical synagogue and you may see the Hebrew letters for Deuteronomy 6:4, *Sh'ma Y'isroel, Adonai elohenu, Adonai ehad*—"Hear [Listen], O Israel, the Lord our God, the Lord is one" [or "the Lord alone"]— and other Hebrew words. God is revealed in words and deeds; to portray visually anything but God's words is to bring God down to our level. Jews honor God through worship and through life.

Jewish worship happens in a synagogue. The Temple has never been rebuilt, and Judaism no longer has priests. While Jews still pray at the Western Wall of the Temple in Jerusalem, rabbis conduct synagogue worship, which includes prayers, singing, readings, and a message. When eight days old, a Jewish baby boy is circumcised in obedience to commandments that extend all the way back to Abraham. Well-known ceremonies called *bar mitzvah* ("son of the commandment") and *bat mitzvah* ("daughter of the commandment") are celebrated for thirteen-year-old boys and girls who have undergone religious training. A ritual bath (*mikvah*) is used for Jewish converts, both men and women, as well as for ritual cleanness (Leviticus 13:15; Numbers 19:31).

Some Jews "keep kosher." According to the Torah (see Leviticus 11), certain animals can be eaten; others are avoided. Animals must be put to death humanely, or else they are not kosher. Some Jews do not

> Read Leviticus 11. Beef and lamb are *kosher* (which means "suitable"), but pork and wild game are forbidden. Domesticated but not wild fowl are suitable. Fish with both gills and scales are suitable, but not fish lacking scales (catfish, for instance) or shellfish. Any edible plants and nuts are suitable. What other creatures are acceptable for consumption? If you were an "observant" Jew (one who observes dietary laws), what kind of menu would you put together?

28

cook dairy and meat in the same utensils, in observance to the commandment (Exodus 23:19; Deuteronomy 14:21). "Do you know what *kashrut* [kosher] is?" Mr. Salzman asked me. "Kosher is not only a religious observance but a matter for health and self-discipline. It is very easy to eat anything. But [keeping] kosher puts you on a straight road."

"And a regard for animals, for the humane slaughter of animals," adds Ms. Foster. "While other cultures would club an animal over the head, for thousands of years Jews killed animals painlessly, with a razor-sharp knife."

"Also blood," said Mr. Salzman, "which is the life of every living thing. So you should not consume blood [out of respect for the animal's life]. According to the law, when you kill an animal the blood has to run out. In the old days, they used to soak the meat in water then apply salt till all the blood disappeared."

The Torah enjoins Jews to practice economic justice and fairness. "There are many laws about fair measure, about giving and paying honestly, about charity," said Ms. Foster. "In America, sociologically Jews are a comfortably well-off group financially—not the most wealthy but certainly middle class. Yet politically Jews have tended to vote on the side of the poor and downtrodden. Jews have always been very concerned with social issues. Although we're not downtrodden ourselves and without civil rights, we stand with and vote with those who are impoverished and lacking in rights, sometimes against our own interests."

Unlike Christian holidays, which arose out of tradition rather than specific, explicit scriptural mandate, the major Jewish holidays are scripturally described (Leviticus 16; 23). *Rosh Hashanah*, or the New Year, begins in

---

For biblical background on the Jewish holidays, read the following Scriptures.

- The Sabbath: Exodus 23:12-13; Leviticus 23:1-2
- Passover: Exodus 12:43-49; Leviticus 4–8
- Shavuot (Pentecost): Leviticus 23:9-22
- Rosh Hashanah: Leviticus 23:9-22
- Yom Kippur: Leviticus 16; 23:26-32
- Sukkoth: Leviticus 23:39-43
- Purim: Esther 9:23-28

According to the Scriptures, what is the meaning of these holidays? What are the recommendations for observing these days? (The historical context for Hanukkah is found in the Apocryphal book of Second Maccabees.)

You might also study the book by Michael Strassfeld, *The Jewish Holidays: A Guide and Commentary* (HarperCollins, 1985).

September. Ten days after New Year, *Yom Kippur*, or "Day of Atonement," allows Jews to begin the year on a fresh spiritual basis. *Sukkoth* in the fall commemorates the forty years of wandering in the wilderness and living in tents. *Pesach,* or Passover, occurs in March or April and commemorates God's salvation of the Hebrews from Egypt. *Shavuot* (Pentecost), a celebration of the wheat harvest seven weeks after the first day of Pesach, developed into a celebration that honors the giving of the Ten Commandments (*Decalog*). Jews observe several minor holidays, two of which are *Purim* and *Hanukkah*. Purim celebrates the deliverance of exiles in Persia from Haman's planned massacre (see the Book of Esther). Hanukkah celebrates Judas Maccabeus's rededication of the Temple after it was polluted by Antiochus Epiphanes.

Serving the World

Do Jews believe in an afterlife? Some do, some do not; the Tanakh has comparatively little to say on the matter. "Judaism is much more geared toward the here and now," says Prof. Silverman. "Yes, there is an afterlife; but you better make sure you're towing the rope *right now*. That's why, every year at Yom Kippur, you reflect upon the past year. What have you done in the past year? What aren't you satisfied with in your life? Are you being a caring person? Are you caring about people who have less than you do? Are you caring for people who need help? That's something that really goes through the religion."

Ms. Foster noted the biblical concept of *sheol*, a shadowy abode of the dead that may or may not be a literal place. According to her "there is very little emphasis in Judaism on the afterlife. At one particularly grim time in history, coincidentally, about the time Christianity started, Jewish theology began to flirt with this idea. Christianity took the concept and ran with it. It has never been an important concept for Judaism, except when Jews have lived among other dominant religions so it rubs off on us. Of course, that's an eternal question: what happens after you die? It's hard to accept that you're buried and go back to earth. But in an important way, you live on in the memory of your loved ones and those you helped."

"The future world is the future generation," says Mr. Salzman. "Nowhere in the [Scriptures] is there anything about the afterlife. It doesn't say, 'I took Moses to me.' It says, 'Moses was buried.' Thus the emphasis on a family. Also, you have to be a good person on this earth. I didn't mistreat people, and I gave to charity as much as I could. Whatever happens then, let someone else judge!"

"Because the concept of afterlife is not emphasized," says Ms. Foster, "the focus is here and now. Because we don't

> What is the Christian view of an afterlife? How does the Christian view affect one's ethical approach to daily life? At what points do the ethics of the Christian view and the Jewish view coincide? At what points do they differ?

have heaven to make up for what we did wrong, we have the chance to do right the first time. Instead of worrying about divine retribution, we try to do it right now. But the question gets posed to rabbis probably the most!"

"Even as a kid," says Prof. Silverman, "when you're bar mitzvahed, one of the things you're asked to do is called *zedaqah* [righteousness]. What are you going to do for your bar mitzvah that's going to help someone—apart from the Temple or school and so on? For instance, my son volunteered at Children's Hospital for a year. It helps you pay attention to the here and now; what

> At this stage of your spiritual life, what kinds of service (that is, serving others, through the church or otherwise) do you enjoy? How do you sacrifice your time in order to serve?

you do may hurt you in the afterlife—whatever that may be—but it's going to hurt you now, too. God is thinking about you now."

"In modern Jewish thinking," says Mr. Salzman, "we are not so much looking toward a messiah but to a messianic age—a time when people get together, get people together, without the hatred we have today. That's the modern interpretation. An age where people will live together and enjoy their days and peace will reign. People will live in good, high standards.

"A human life takes precedence in Judaism," he continued. "To save a human life, regardless of who is it, is like saving the whole world. If it is Saturday or Yom Kippur, and there is an emergency, you use whatever means of transportation to get them to the hospital. Shabbat is not for God. The Shabbat is to get your mind clear and your body rested."

> Form teams of two or three. Recall your work earlier in this lesson when you brainstormed all the things you could think of concerning Jews and Judaism. Now that you have read the lesson, what insights have you gained? How has your mind changed? What remains the same?

31

A Jewish View of Other Faiths

What is the Jewish view of other faiths? "Maybe it's because we're nearly always a minority, you have to respect other faiths! Nobody has captured the corner on religion," says Prof. Silverman. "I respect every religion," says Mr. Salzman. "The only thing I don't respect is when someone tries to convince me that their religion is better than mine. You should live your life according to the basic principles of monotheistic religion. There is so much similarity, for instance, among Judaism, Christianity, and Islam. You have to have faith to believe."

Closing
Close with a unison recitation of Psalm 150.

For More Information
Look for books about Judaism that can help deepen your understanding.

• *Tanakh: The Holy Scriptures* is a Jewish Bible translation that does not rely upon Christian Old Testament translations. Philadelphia: Jewish Publication Society, 1988.
• Rabbi Wayne Dosick, *Living Judaism: The Complete Guide to Jewish Belief, Tradition, and Practice.* San Francisco: HarperSanFrancisco, 1995.
• Daniel C. Matt, *The Essential Kabbalah: The Heart of Jewish Mysticism.* San Francisco: HarperSanFrancisco, 1996.
• Bruce Feiler, *Walking the Bible: A Journey by Land Through the Five Books of Moses.* New York: William Morrow & Co., 2001.
• Alfred J. Kolatch, *The Jewish Book of Why* (Middle Village, NY: Jonathan David Publishers, 1981), and *The Second Jewish Book of Why* (same publisher, 1985). These books answer many common questions about Judaism.
• A harrowing book about the Nazi genocide of Jews, among other good histories, is Christopher R. Browning, *Ordinary Men: Reserve Police Battalion 101 and the Final Solution in Poland.* New York: Harper Perennial, 1993, 1998.

CHAPTER 3
NO GOD BUT GOD

Islam

Dear God – As we study about these different faiths – Help us to recognize the similarities that could bind us together and understand that the differences need not separate us. So we recognize that we here also have many differences but the beliefs that we have that are the same bind us together in understanding & friendship and the differences stimulate us to search our hearts. Help us to be open to these new understandings, in God's name we ask this. – Amen

Religious Neighbors

"Most people don't see the good sides of Islam!" says Mohammad al-Sharif, a Jerusalem-born graduate student at the University of Akron who often finds himself explaining Islam to his coworkers at an Akron-area business. "People see only what the media says, that Islam promotes killing, and so on. What's going on with radical Muslims today has to do with politics, with the economy, with the particular region—but it doesn't represent the whole of Islam. You try to tell people, though, and the

Focus: This session explores key doctrines and practices of Islam.

Gathering

Greet one another and welcome any new-comers. Share highlights of your lives since you last met. Offer to God any world situations in which Muslims and non-Muslims are in conflict.

Brainstorm all the things that come to your mind when you think of "Islam" and "Muslims." What about the religion do you not understand?

Study newspapers and news magazines to see how Islam is portrayed in the media. If you had only the media to go on, what would be your impression of Islam? Would your impression be primarily negative, positive, or in between? Also think about movies you've seen in which Muslims and/or Arabs have been portrayed. What impression comes through to you?

33

> What words come to your mind when you think of *submission* or *surrender*? Are they positive or negative images? How is submission to God a positive image?
>
> Some Christian sermons and hymns refer to religious submission. (The old hymn "I Surrender All" comes to mind.) Discuss the concept. Does religious submission mean the same thing as passivity in the face of life's challenges? Does it mean strength in time of trouble? What is required to surrender yourself to God?

answer is much bigger than they expected."

"Islam," he pointed out to me, "means 'submission' to God—it is related to the word for 'peace'—and a Muslim is one who has 'submitted' to God." Islam is the only major world religion established since the beginning of Christianity. In numbers Islam ranks a close second behind Christianity, with more than a billion adherents in the world.

> People sometimes confuse the terms *Muslim* and *Arab*. *Muslim* is a religious term, while *Arab* is an ethnic term describing persons from or descended from persons from Arabia. Although the word *Semite* is often used just for Jews, Jews and Arabs, as well as some other Middle Eastern groups, are all *Semitic*.

Allah

Allah is the Arabic word that translates into "the God," and it carries the understanding that God is the one and only God. He is the same God worshiped by Jews and Christians. He is not "Father" but he is our Sovereign and Lord. As the Qur'an begins, "Praise be to Allah, the Cherisher and Sustainer of the Worlds; Most Gracious, Most Merciful; Master of the Day of Judgment. Thee do we worship, and Thine aid we seek."

The author Solomon Nigosian (in his book cited on page 44, pages 142–44) lists the ninety-nine "beautiful names" of God in the Muslim tradition. Some are positive, loving names: Compassionate, Merciful, Source of Peace, Protector, Creator, Forgiver, Gracious, Generous, Liberal, Wise, Praiseworthy,

> Think about Islam's "beautiful names of Allah." Make your own list of God's names, either biblical names or names that describe God's attributes. How do these names clarify God's nature to you?

(adjectives mostly)

Master
Father
Creator
Lord

34

Amply Beneficient, Acceptor of repentance, Kindly, Enricher, and Patient. Other names warn of God's righteousness: Judge, Just, Reckoner, Abaser, Avenger, and Depriver. He is the Great in Majesty, Most High, Giver of life and Giver of death, All-Knowing, Guide and Director. As Mr. Tayeh noted in my interview, all these are preceded with the definite article "The" emphasizing the supremacy of God.

God's Nature

Raeed Tayeh, a government relations specialist with the Muslim American Society and author of *A Muslim's Guide to American Politics and Government*, has discussed Islam on several news programs like MSNBC's *Hardball*, FOX's *O'Reilly's Factor*, C-SPAN, and Al Jazeera. A person with ties to northeast Ohio, he explained God's characteristics as revealed to humans. "Allah is not human, thus He is neither male nor female in the human sense. However, He refers to Himself in the Qur'anic text in the masculine form. None has come before Him, and none will come after Him."

The nature of God is clearly seen in how God deals with human sin. "Sin is the disobedience of Allah," says Mr. Tayeh. "Engaging in acts that are forbidden, or *harram*, are sins. We know what is harram from what Allah has revealed to us in the Qur'an and from what the Prophet Muhammad has taught us through his speech, actions, and opinions. Every sane human becomes accountable for their sins once they reach puberty. Children, and those who have no control over their minds, are exempt from judgment. Everyone has two angels accompanying him or her at all times, one on each shoulder. The angel on the right shoulder records one's good deeds, and the angel on the left shoulder records one's bad sins.

"Allah's scales are clearly imbalanced, in favor of humans. For every good deed committed, God will multiply its worth from anywhere between 10 to 700 times. Even if one plans to do a good deed, but for some reason they don't, they still get the reward of their intentions.

"Sins are not multiplied and are recorded at face value. One has not committed sin if they contemplated doing something bad, but didn't actually do it. Thus Allah is truly the Most Merciful because if we apply this to the human justice system, there is no such leniency."

Prophets and Messengers

God has spoken through a number of prophets and "messengers" over the centuries, including those esteemed by Jews and Christians. The Qur'an (for example, 6:83-90) mentions several prophets and messengers, including Old and New Testament figures such as Adam, Abraham, Moses, Aaron, David, Solomon, and others, as well as Zechariah and John the Baptist. Earlier Scriptures given by God are the Scrolls, a lost scripture that Abraham received; the Torah, the revelation given to Moses; the scriptures given to David, another prophet; and the Gospels, given to Jesus.[1] In each of these cases, people had, intentionally or unintentionally, made errors in the texts or had interpreted the texts wrongly.[2]

For Muslims, Jesus is a prophet miraculously born of a virgin. The Qur'an honors Mary, Jesus' mother, as an example of great faith. Jesus, however, was not crucified; another man substituted for him. "People ask me, 'Do you believe in Jesus?' " says Mr. al-Sharif. "Yes, I do. The difference is I believe he is a prophet. We believe he was born without a father. We have respect for him and his mother and for other prophets in other religions." According to Mr. al-Sharif, Adam was born

---

> • **Prophet** (in Arabic, *nabi*) one whom God calls to warn and guide persons as to God's will. God gives revelations to human beings through a prophet, one who has surrendered fully to God. Thus God appoints that prophet to warn and guide persons as to God's word and will.
>
> • **Messenger** (*rasool* in Arabic): one through whom God gives *written* revelation. All messengers are prophets but not all prophets are messengers. Muhammad is properly called a prophet and a messenger.[3]

> Think about the idea of *prophet*. What would qualify a person to be entrusted with a special message from God? How would you expect people to treat that person? Would the prophet be accepted? persecuted? What would you, personally, do if you were persecuted for your faith?
>
> Think of persons in history, in addition to the prophet Muhammad, who received poor treatment in response to their preaching. Examples might include Joseph Smith (a prophet of the Mormon tradition), Dr. Martin Luther King Jr., the apostle Paul, and others. What happened to these people? How do we use the word *prophet* in both specialized and nonspecialized ways?

without a human father and mother, while Jesus was born without a human father. In both cases the births were miraculous, but neither Adam nor Jesus should be considered divine or a Son of God. Muslims believe Jesus will return to earth to lead the righteous and destroy the false prophet.

> Think of your spiritual journey as a "road trip." What has kept you on the straight way? What made you detour, get lost, or break down on the roadside?

personal concerns self-grandize ment

The Qur'an

The Qur'an is the final message from God to help humankind conform to God's will; it offers the "the straight path." Muslims do not believe in original sin or an inherent flaw in our spiritual being. Rather, we have free will. We can be taught to follow God more closely and to rely upon God's mercy. Sometimes we choose to do wrong; other times we are forgetful and careless of our responsibilities to God. Thus another word for Islam is "the straight path" by which God directs us.

The Qur'an is about the length of the New Testament; it consists of 114 "suras," which basically means sections. The Qur'an is written in a highly literary style. The suras are arranged in order from the longest to the shortest. How do we know the Qur'an is God's word? Muhammad, God's last prophet, was a man of integrity; he was also illiterate. The Qur'an is written in extremely fine Arabic and indeed is a model of Arabic language, far better, Muslims believe, than could have originated from mere human authorship. One must hear it and read it in Arabic to fully appreciate the rhythms and sounds that carry meaning along with the meaning of the words.

Muslims respect Jews and Christians as "people of the Book"—a positive Qur'an expression that indicates that Jews and Christians (1) believe in one God and (2) believe that God has been revealed verbally and God's words can be read and heeded. "I watch the news a lot and some of those religious channels," noted Mr. al-Sharif. "It's a problem, because most of those churches do not accept Islam as a [true] religion. But in the opposite way, Islam accepts Christianity and Judaism." Muslims recognize no other religions as true, however. For Muslims the worst sins are "shirk" (idolatry, which means setting any earthly thing before God or as a representation of God) and the related sin of polytheism (worshiping more than one God).

37

Muhammad and the Origins of Islam

Muhammad is God's final prophet. He was born about A.D. 570 in Arabia to a prosperous family. Orphaned at a young age, he was raised by relatives. Although he could not read or write, he gained a reputation for honesty and integrity in his work. Although Muslims do not revere Muhammad as a savior, which would be a blasphemy against God, who alone is savior, Muslims honor and revere Muhammad as an exemplary human being of wisdom, integrity, and compassion. He married a woman named Khadijah, who was born about A.D. 555. They had four daughters but no sons who lived beyond infancy.

When he was a young man, Muhammad often retreated to the desert and mountains to pray. During one of these solitary times, the angel Gabriel appeared to him and demanded that he recite. Beginning in 610 and for the next twenty-two years, Muhammad received revelations from God that were subsequently written down by his companions.

The Qur'an is considered God's eternal word but also relates to particular circumstances during Muhammad's life. Muhammad received poor treatment from the people of his hometown, Mecca, in what is now western Saudi Arabia. In addition to his difficulties, the Prophet lost his beloved wife, who had greatly encouraged him, when she died in 619. A few years later he also lost his uncle who had raised him and subsequently had accorded him protection. Another uncle became clan leader and refused to protect Muhammad; thus he could no longer preach lest he be attacked. In 622, Muhammad led other Muslims to a different city, Medina, where the Muslims were welcomed and accepted into leadership. Year 1 of the Muslim calendar is 622, the year of the migration or *hijrah* to Medina. In Medina, the Prophet first established Islamic law. By 630, the Muslims returned to Mecca in triumph. Muhammad established a government according to God's laws, removed pagan images from the *Ka'bah*, the cubical temple in Mecca said to be built by Abraham, and led the Muslims until his death in 632.

In the decades following Muhammad's death, the faith spread quickly through a process of evangelization and military conquest. By the middle of the 700s, Arabia, Palestine, and North Africa had become Muslim. Because Muhammad had named no successor and had no son who would automatically have succeeded him, Muslims split between two "factions." The Sunnis elected the leader, who was called the Caliph, according to the tradition established immediately after the Prophet died. The Shi'ites desired the Muslim leadership to stay within the Prophet's family. Today Shi'ites account for about 10 percent of all Muslims and primarily live in Iran, Iraq, and some other countries. Sunnis believe that God's revelation, the gift of prophetic teaching, ended with Muhammad. Shi'ites believe that certain special teachers or *imams* are divinely endowed special interpreters of God's world. Shi'ites honor Muhammad's daughter Fatima, his son-in-law Ali, and Ali's son Husein, as well as other members of the Prophet's family, as great heroes and, in the case of several family members, as martyrs.

Islam's "classical period," the seventh through the thirteenth centuries, featured tremendous growth west and east, development of Islamic law (*Shari'ah*) and theology, and the growth of the mystical Sufi movement. Although from the fifteenth through the nineteenth centuries several Muslim empires including the Ottoman continued, events such as the Crusades and the Mongol invasions disrupted important Muslim areas, as did later Western colonization and modernization. Since the nineteenth century, movements of reform and renewal have occurred in many parts of the Muslim world, including modernization in some countries and traditionalist movements in others.

Muslim Beliefs

A Muslim friend says there is no "typical" kind of Muslim, just as there is no "typical" Christian. Even the Qur'an is open to many interpretations, and Muslims expect that it should be interpreted and struggled over. But Islam does have several constants. We have already touched upon several: the oneness and nature of God, God's compassion for sinners, the purpose of the prophets, the essential scripture, the Muslim view of other religions.

What is the basis of forgiveness? Mr. Tayeh says, "One has until the last breath taken into their body to repent to Allah for sins committed. If one commits sin, sincerely repents, and does their best to not repeat the sin, then that sin will be erased from the angel's books. The only sin that is unforgivable to Allah is polytheism, or associating others with Allah . . . if one dies without believing in God, and, furthermore, believing in other Gods, then he or she is doomed.

"In addition to repentance, there are many ways that Muslims way seek forgiveness for their sins. Performing the *Hajj* with sincere intentions will wipe away all one's sins. Fasting the entire month of Ramadan will also do it. What is clear from the guidelines is that there is heavy emphasis on inten-

> What are your "pillars of faith"? In other words, what supports your religious life and growth? How many pillars do you have? Which of your pillars are inner-directed (personal religious growth) and which are outer-directed (service to others)? How do the individual and the social elements of your own pillars work together? Describe your daily/weekly disciplines if you practice them. Do you pray or read Scripture at certain times? Do you fast, or study particular works? What disciplines might you add to your daily life?

tions, both before and after the fact. In Islam, every act committed with a good intention is considered as worship to Allah. Allah does not need our worship, but we do need it to earn His pleasure with our deeds. The Prophet Muhammad once said, 'Even smiling at your brother is charity.' "

Mr. Tayeh explained the Muslim worship and ethical demands. "There are mandatory acts of worship, some physical, some spiritual, that are required of Muslims. The physical acts are: (1) to declare that there is no God but Allah, and that Muhammad is His messenger, (2) to perform the five daily prayers, (3) to pay the annual *zakat*, or 2.5 percent of one's wealth to charity, (4) to fast the holy month of Ramadan (if able), and (5) to perform the Hajj, or pilgrimage to Mecca at least once (if physically and financially able). These are known as the Pillars of Islam. The spiritual acts of worship are: (1) to believe in the oneness of Allah, (2) to believe in all of Allah's prophets, from Adam to Muhammad, including Moses and Jesus, (3) to believe in Allah's revealed books (the Torah, Psalms, Gospels, and Qur'an, though Muslims follow the Qur'an as the final text), (4) to believe in Allah's angels, (5) to believe in the Day of Judgment, and (6) to believe in destiny, and Allah's power to exert His will freely."

> Visit a mosque. Call to find times when the imam (teacher) or some other host can guide you through the facility.

Many Muslims, in addition to practicing the five pillars, abstain from pork and alcohol. Muslims differ as to whether deviation from the five pillars removes one, at least temporarily, from the Muslim "community." For instance, some Muslims say you are absolutely obliged to pay your zakat; others will be more tolerant of different practices.

> What are the ethical standards that you follow in your spiritual walk?

"Muslims have a personal, as well

as social, responsibility to behave in the highest moral standard possible," Mr. Tayeh continued. "Man is in a constant struggle with the devil, who has sworn to do everything possible to misguide humans to prove that they are not worthy of blessings that Allah has bestowed upon them. Islam demands that you constantly engage in the internal personal struggle of *jihad*, in order to overcome weaknesses in faith that may lead one to cheat, lie, fornicate, or even disbelieve."

In Muslim belief, in Mr. Tayeh's words, "when one dies, one enters the second phase of life, so to speak, and one's soul enters the grave. The grave gives one a good indication of what his or her ultimate fate might be like. For one who committed many unforgiving sins, the grave will be a torturous and wretched place. For a righteous person, the grave will be a part of heaven, and the waiting period to the Day of Judgment will go quickly. All humans will stand before God on the Day of Judgment and be held accountable for their actions in their human life based on what they knew of right and wrong. If their sins outweigh their good deeds, their fate will be hellfire for a set time or perhaps even forever. If one's good deeds outweigh the sins, then his or her fate is eternal paradise. The Qur'an describes heaven as 'Gardens from which underneath rivers flow' in several locations, and it also describes the four rivers from which paradise dwellers will drink; rivers of water, honey, yogurt, and wine (described in the Qur'an as sweet wine from Allah, unlike the earthly one that makes one's head ache)."

Thinking about the afterlife, Mr. al-Sharif notes, "Many people worship in order to get to heaven or to avoid hell. But some people say, 'No, I'm not interested in going to hell or interested in being in heaven. I want to know God for the love of God, for knowing God in love, for spreading love.' To me, it is a more accurate way to worship God, through love rather than through fear. I think love will give you more understanding of everything around you. Not to get rid of the rules and regulations, but love helps you understand things more. From the fear point of view, you have no choice. From the love point of view, you understand better why."

Muslim Law

God's law trains people in righteousness, in disciplining one's heart, and in struggling (*jihad*) against one's baser nature. The word *jihad* can mean "holy war" in a political sense, but the "true war" is against one's lower nature as one struggles spiritually and morally to grow closer to God.

41

175 led by the spirit *215* *p 181 their due pay (taxes)* *218*

> What defines a Christian's freedom? Read Galatians 5:16-24; Romans 8:1-27; Romans 13:6-7; and Ephesians 4:17–5:20. For Paul, what is a Christian's guide for ethical behavior? What "safeguards" does a Christian have to know that he or she is actually following the Spirit? What are the bases not only for individual morality but also a just and righteous society? What other Scriptures could help you form an answer?

Muslim law is called *Shari'ah*. Shari'ah develops from two primary sources. The chief source is the Qur'an. Another is the *hadith*, or the traditions and sayings of the prophet Muhammad alluded to above by Mr. Tayeh. Muhammad's interpretations of the Qur'an, and his decisions and examples as he governed the early Muslims, have been preserved over the centuries. The *hadith* do not carry the same weight as the Qur'an, but this material is very important in developing Muslim laws.

Mr. al-Sharif notes, "Islam defines your freedom—even where your freedom stops and the other person's starts. Islam defines how respect is built in between your wife, your neighbor, your parents, even how the society is structured. If you break laws, this is the consequence. So the whole society is connected, like one body, so that if one person behaves badly, this is the punishment. You have your freedom, but there is a limitation on freedom.

"[In the Shari'ah] there are even rules about how to take care of the family. Even the Prophet, when he came around to play with his grandkids, everybody said, 'The Prophet isn't supposed to relate to kids.' But the Prophet, like any other grandparent, wanted to play with the kids! People don't see that lovely side of Islam. . . ."

He adds, "There's a school in religion that talks about the mystical in Islam, higher knowing and learning from God. You have to work a lot for it, by purifying yourself, by fighting the devil within you, which is called in Islam, *Jihad akbar*, which means the 'greater struggle.' You're always fighting against your nature."

> Recall your work earlier in this session when you brainstormed all the things you could think of concerning Islam and Muslims. Now that you have read the chapter, what insights have you gained? What in your thinking has changed? What has remained the same?

Legacy

Do you use Arabic numbers instead of

Roman numerals? Thank mathematicians from the Muslim world! Over the centuries Muslims also gave to the world innovations in the areas of science, medicine, literature, textiles, art, and architecture. Works of ancient Greek philosophers became known to late medieval Christian thinkers through the translations and commentaries of Muslim scholars, in particular the philosopher and scholar Averroës. These works profoundly shaped Christian thought.

Many other positive legacies have come from the Muslim world, including models of interreligious tolerance. When Spain was predominantly Islamic, exemplary tolerance was accorded to Jews, which contrasted to the intolerance shown Jews and Muslims by later, Christian Spain. When you look into all the good sides of Islam, as Mr. al-Sharif says, the answer is much bigger than expected!

Closing

Close your time with this reading from the Qur'an (2:177), from the 1964 Oxford University Press translation: "It is not piety, that you turn your faces / to the East and to the West. / True piety is this: / to believe in God, and the Last Day, / the angels, the Book, and the Prophets, / to give of one's substance, however cherished, / to kinsmen, and orphans, / the needy, the traveller, beggars, / and to ransom the slave, / to perform the prayer, to pay the alms. / And they who fulfill their covenant / when they have engaged in a covenant, / and endure with fortitude / misfortune, hardship and peril, / these are they who are true in their faith, / these are the truly godfearing."

Notes

1. Solomon Nigosian, *Islam: The Way of Submission* (Great Britain: Crucible, 1987), page 111. Also Suzanne Haneef, *What Everybody Should Know About Islam and Muslims* (DesPlaines, IL: Library of Islam, 1993), page 21.

2. Ibid., page 118. Nigosian points out several Christian beliefs the Muslims consider erroneous: God as Father, human beings as God's children, the divinity of Jesus, the Trinity, and the holiness of the church.

3. Haneef, page 20.

For More Information

Look for books about Islam that can help deepen your understanding.

• *The Holy Qur'an: Text, Translation and Commentary.* Edited by Abdullah Yusuf Ali. Brentwood, MD: Amana Corporation, 1989.
• Solomon Nigosian, *Islam: The Way of Submission.* New York: HarperCollins, 1987.
• Francis E. Peters, *Children of Abraham: Judaism, Christianity, Islam.* Princeton: Princeton University Press, 1982, and the same author's *Islam: A Guide for Jews and Christians.* Princeton: 2003.
• Suzanne Haneef, *What Everybody Should Know About Islam and Muslims.* Des Plaines, IL: Library of Islam, 1993.

• Also check out *www.cair-net.org* and *www.islam.com.*

CHAPTER 4
DIFFERENT STREAMS
TOWARD ONE RIVER

1/3/06

Hinduism

A "Decentralized" Faith

Focus: This session explores the world-views and traditions of Hinduism.

"Don't give that hippie your money!" my father declared, misidentifying a Hare Krishna person selling sticks of incense for a quarter in downtown St. Louis in the early 1970s. To one who knows little about Hinduism, the name may elicit particular images: Hare Krishna people, yoga, reincarnation, "sacred cows," Gandhi, George Harrison songs, and the caste system—in other words, images drawn from the media but no real in-depth knowledge.

Gathering
After the group assembles, think about the things you'd like to learn about Hinduism. Be open to new discoveries about your own faith as you study Hinduism.
Tell about things that have been unusual or unique about the week just past. Share prayer concerns and praises.

Those approaching Hinduism for a more complete examination may find the faith daunting at first. Hinduism has one divine spirit, yet it has many deities. It has many scriptures, yet particular ones are considered more sacred than others.

What has been your firsthand experience of Hinduism, if any? Do a word association game. Make a list of everything that comes to mind when you hear the word *Hinduism*.

Look in the Yellow Pages at the varieties of Christian denominations in your city or region. How do you discern among different Christian "belief systems"? What Christian practices have been "picked up" over history, that is, things that are important but not mentioned in the Bible?

Which do you think has the greater impact, a "grassroots" movement started by many people, working together and spreading news mouth to mouth, or a movement begun by a particular dynamic leader? What are the plusses and minuses of both kinds of movements? Who do you consider an authority figure in Christianity today? Is he or she an authority figure to you?

One may practice Hinduism in a variety of ways: worship of a particular god, physical and spiritual exercises, responsible attention to one's duties, reading, and silent nonverbal meditation. Some Hindus even renounce all that they have in order to live completely devoted to God.

Dr. Surinder M. Bhardwaj, professor of cultural geography/India at the department of geography at Kent State University, is the author of a classic on its subject, *Hindu Places of Pilgrimage in India: A Study in Cultural Geography* (Berkeley: University of California Press, 1983). Dr. Bhardwaj sat down with me one day, made me tea, and explained several aspects of Hinduism. "Hinduism seems quite complex," he said, "in part because it is not an organized religion in the same way as Christianity or Islam or Sikhism. There is no one single focus, no single originator of the faith about which there is consensus. Hinduism is a flow of different streams toward one large river. A large number of belief systems, a large number of thought patterns, have merged together to create what is now Hinduism. As all religions evolve, present-day Hinduism is quite different from Hinduism of the classical times and the ancient times."

Hinduism has been called a "decentralized" faith because of

• **Syncretism**: combining different beliefs and practices from different sources.

its lack of a founder and a single authority. It is also very syncretistic. Thus one finds wide varieties of Hindu belief and practice but without the vying claims for higher truth found, for instance, among Christian denominations.

runs into Bombay

Historical Origins

The Sanskrit word *Sindhu* refers to the Indus River. *Hindu* is a Persian word referring to the people who lived near the Indus River. Hindus themselves call their faith *sanatana dharma*, or the eternal dharma. Hinduism began about 4,000 years ago among the people of the Indus River Valley. Eventually this civilization merged with Aryan people. *Aryan* designates a particular people originating in central Asia who subsequently migrated to India. Some of the deities, religious iconography, and scriptural traditions originated during the second millennium B.C. "As the population of people expanded and more of the Ganges Plain began to be populated," says Dr. Bhardwaj, "the religion with its variants began to diffuse and absorbed many of the belief patterns that were prevalent there earlier

---

Hindu Scriptures

Among the several Hindu scriptures, some of the most important ones include:

• The *Vedas* (developed and compiled about 1500–200 B.C.), which in turn has four parts:

Samhitas: hymns to the gods and cosmic forces, including the Rig Veda, which, according to some Hindus, dates from the 6000s B.C. and earlier

poetry

Brahmanas: scriptures about sacrifices

Aranyakas: the "forest treatises"

Upanishads: poems concerning ultimate reality, samsara, and liberation

• *Dharma Sutras* (compiled during the first two centuries A.D.): describes the castes or classes of society

• *Ramayana* (compiled during the "classical era"): an epic poem about the heroism of the prince Rama and, in a greater sense, the victory of Vishnu over evil forces

• *Mahabharata* (compiled during the classical era): another epic poem concerning the rivalries within the Pandava family and, in a greater sense, the nature of dharma and bhakti

• *Puranas* (compiled about A.D. 300s–800s): stories about the gods in the devotional (bhakti) tradition.[1]

In a retreat setting, study some Hindu scriptures together. A good selection of this material can be found in *A Sourcebook in Indian Philosophy,* edited by Sarvepalli Radhakrishnan and Charles A. Moore (Princeton University Press, 1957, 1989).

---

among the tribal folk, the forest dwellers, and others. The Aryan way of life and pre-Aryan way of life began to fuse together."

Recently, theories that the Aryan civilization superseded the indigenous Indus Valley culture has been disputed by Hindus and historians alike. Research into the connection between Vedic religion, the Aryan peoples, and the Indus Valley civilization is ongoing.

The chief Hindu scriptures emerged from this early time—about 1500 B.C. Developing from Aryan and Indus valley traditions, the *Vedas* (pronounced VAY-dahs) are hymns in honor of gods, songs for sacrifices, and hymns for other religious occasions. The word Veda means "knowledge." Some of the early *Vedas* include the *Rig Veda* from the thirteenth century B.C., the *Samhitas*, the *Brahmanas*, and the *Upanishads* from the sixth century B.C. and later. The *Vedas* are called *Shruti,* "what has been heard"—that is, the *Vedas* originate from the gods and thus cannot be changed or altered. Most Hindus revere the *Vedas* as the primary scriptures, though these scriptures are not typically read and consulted by most Hindus.

During the period of "classical Hinduism" (400 B.C. till A.D. 400), other scriptures were compiled called the *Smriti.* The Smriti were passed down orally but not word for word. Among other scriptures, including the *Yoga Sutras* and *Dharma Sutras,* this period saw two epic poems compiled. The first was the *Ramayana,* the hero of which is Rama, an incarnation of the deity Vishnu. The second was the *Mahabharata,* an epic poem of 100,000 lines that concerns the rivalry of two great Indian families. The *Mahabharata* also addresses the religious themes of *dharma, bhakti,* and *moksha.* The *Bhagavad-Gita,* at 700 verses, is a very small portion of the *Mahabharata.* But the *Bhagavad-Gita* is a very popular and widely published scripture in its own right. The word *bhakti* means devotion to a particular deity, and the A.D. 400–1800 period of Hinduism saw a great flowering of bhakti practices and traditions. Still other scriptural traditions, called the *Puranas,* developed during this period. More recently, the past two centuries have seen reform movements within Hinduism including modifications of the old caste system and new spiritual movements.

> Draw a picture of how you interpret the universe. Include both the "objective" reality and the moral and spiritual reality in which you believe.

Worldview

In a study of Hinduism, we start with the worldview that includes ethical and religious demands, the consequences of dishonoring those demands, and the concept of the afterlife. Then we examine the concept of God.

For nearly all Hindus, reality is explained by the

> How has your faith changed over time? How did you relate to God as a child? as an adolescent? as an adult? What has been the interplay between your faith and your social, professional, and family responsibilities?

interrelated, spiritual and moral concepts of *dharma, karma, samsara, moksha,* and *Brahman. Dharma* refers to a person's social duties and responsibilities. As Dr. Bhardwaj explained to me, my dharma as a husband, my dharma as a father, my dharma as a teacher are different and have evolved over time. My dharma as a young son of my father was different from my dharma when I was an adult and he an old man. Not only that, but my dharma includes my responsibilities in my profession and my place in society. Everyone has particular duties to fulfill, depending upon his or her life stage or position in society. In traditional Indian thinking, persons are obliged to have children. Persons are obliged to eat particular foods and abstain from others. Hindus do not eat beef, for instance.

> Think of times when you did something, good or bad, which had unexpected repercussions. What happened? What did you learn from the experience? What actions in your life have most affected you, for good or ill? Have you ever used the expression *karma* informally, especially when one event led unexpectedly to another, or when events, usually bad or inconvenient, started to "pile up" on you? What were the circumstances?

Persons should also work in their job in an honest, honorable manner.

Dharma is tied with the notion of *karma. Karma* is the moral law of cause and effect. Every action has repercussions on both the physical and the spiritual world. We certainly know that our actions have consequences, for good and ill. These consequences, though, follow us as our souls are reborn following the death of our physical bodies. "Bad" karma ties us to the cycle of rebirth and thus delays our return to God. "Good" karma brings us closer to liberation from rebirth. Works of dharma, worship, and in some cases renunciation can bring us closer to liberation.

"My karma appears in light of my dharma," says Dr. Bhardwaj. "My actions appear in light of my duty. Inappropriate actions bind me to the

> How do the ideas of cycle of rebirth and reincarnation compare to the Christian notion of the soul?

earth and to the cycle of rebirth, until I realize that my purpose is to be with Brahman. That realization is *moksha*, or liberation. Ultimately Hindus believe that is their goal: to achieve liberation from the fact of karma, to realize and recognize one's identity with the universal spirit. There may be some souls who realize their identity with the universal spirit while they are in the phenomenal world, whereas others probably have to come back again and again to achieve that realization. That realization is ultimately the goal, as I understand it."

> Christians speak of liberation from sin, and of Jesus "taking away" sin. How do you understand these ideas? What similarities or differences do you see between them and the Hindu concepts of karma and dharma?

Samsara refers to the cycles of rebirth in the universe. As texts on Hinduism explain, time is not linear, with a beginning and an end, but is cyclical, like a wheel. Yet Hindus believe that time does wind down toward an end. Time has moved away from the past "golden age" toward *Kali Yuga*, the present time, which will end in a cataclysm. But then a new *Krita Yuga* or "golden age" will arise again, and so on.

When one achieves moksha, one returns to the universal spirit, or *Brahman*. Brahman is the sacred, eternal spirit outside time and space. Brahman is not a personal God, nor a "being" with attributes, but rather is the source and power of the cosmos manifested in the phenomenal world. According to the scriptures called the *Upanishads,* the soul or *atman* is not an aspect of our individuality but is really the universal spirit itself. Rather than saying our souls are some personal spiritual quality, some Hindus believe our

> Which of the following biblical points of view best reflects your belief? Why? What connections, if any, do you see between these points of view and the Hindu ideas of dharma and karma?
>
> 1. Allegiance to Jesus supersedes all worldly duties and relationships (Matthew 10:34-39).
>
> 2. Allegiance to Jesus means you should take worldly duties and relationships all the more seriously (Ephesians 5:22–6:4).

souls are already one with God. Other Hindus differentiate the soul from the Supreme Spirit, for on earth our spirits are engulfed by illusion or *maya*, which our spirits must break through.

Drawing parallels between Hinduism and Christianity, one might say that "sin" is not only deviation from dharma, as well as indifference to karmic cycles, but also a failure to recognize that all reality is actually one. "Forgiveness" is tied in with one's karma as well, not as a slate being wiped clean, but of a closer proximity to one's ultimate moksha.

liberation

The Caste System

Originally in Indian society there were three *varnas*, or social groups: the priests (Brahman), *Kshatriyas* (warriors), and *Vaishyas* (merchants and others). Later the *Shudra* class, the servants, developed from the three varnas. Still later another varna, the *Harijan* caste of "untouchables" was added. Ghandi popularized the name *Harijan*; another name is *Dalit*, or the oppressed. *Dalit* actually means "ground down." Within these varnas are many *jatis* or castes.[2] In modern times the caste system has been criticized and modified. There are also four life stages (*ashramas*): students (*brahmachari*), householders, and the *sannyasi* or world renouncer. If one chooses the path of the *sannyasin*, one gives up all worldly identities in order to devote oneself completely to meditation.[3] Each life stage in turn has particular dharmas: worldly success (artha), happiness or pleasure (kama), and upright behavior (dharma).[4]

Death and Life

One's individuality—one's personal identity—is something not to be prized. Nor is one's individuality part of one's essential nature. When we achieve moksha, we return to that which we really are, God. "There is nothing that is not God—that is what most Hindus today believe," says Dr. Bhardwaj. "Really only God is; the rest of it is manifestation of the spirit that totally pervades everything. Personally I feel very much a part of the universe. I feel literally connected all the time. I'm not just an identity but also a part of that universal spirit. I feel very connected with the cosmos."

> How do you feel connected to the cosmos? What things help you feel close to God's world? to God?

In Christianity, how do we experience assurance of salvation? Do you think salvation is always connected to feelings of conversion and assurance? Why or why not?

Can one know in a particular life that one has reached moksha? According to Dr. Bhardwaj, most people will only strive for it in this life; but for a few persons, he or she might have a perception of liberation. The achievement, though, keeps people striving for liberation—if not in this life, perhaps in the next.

"Death is not the end of something," he explains, "but rather a stage in the progression of the spirit. Death is of the body, the material substance of which we are made, but death is not of the spirit. Our spirit is that universal spirit, and thus it cannot die. Death is only the destruction of our present form. Hindus grieve as much as anyone, of course; but their solace comes from the fact that death is only a stage in the progression of the spirit. This individual identity is only an ephemeral thing in the first place.

"The very fact of coming back to life and coming back through the various aspects of life—trauma, pain, and so on—that in itself is something Hindus want to rise above. Thus the effort is to break the cycle of return to the phenomenal world. How to break the cycle becomes an important activity. One of the ways is to do the right actions. The path of action. Another might be the path of realization. One path might be more suitable for one kind of individual than another; a contemplative individual might be more apt to follow the path of realization while a more practical individual might be more apt to follow the path of action. There are many other paths. It is possible, following a particular path, ultimately to recognize one's identity with the universal spirit."

Striving Toward Moksha: God, Ethics, and Worship

Hinduism offers several particular paths believers may follow. One is simply the path of dharma. Hindus may approach the universal spirit through carrying out one's social responsibilities. The *Bhagavad-Gita* develops this insight a step further. If one acts with selfless motives, renouncing desire for worldly success as

Compare the ideas of dharma, karma, and moksha to the Western religious ideas of sin, forgiveness, hell, and heaven. What are the similarities and differences?

well as certain outcomes of our actions, one can advance even further toward moksha.

Some Hindus approach the universal spirit through yogic practices. Many popular books have been published about yoga, by model Christy Turlington and others. In Hinduism there are actually four kinds of yoga. *Raja yoga* is the employment of physical exercises and postures (called *asanas*) combined with nonverbal meditation. Raja yoga "taps" the *kundalini*, or the energy found in one's energy points or *pranas*. *Jnana yoga* concentrates specifically on the ignorance of the mind—the mind's inability to see the soul (*atman*) is really God (*Brahman*). In *karma yoga*, one provides help and service to people, but not with consideration of results or return. This kind of yoga is taught in the *Bhagavad Gita*. *Bhakti yoga* is the kind of yoga practiced by most Hindus: showing devotion to one's favorite god or gods.[5]

Yoga, which means "yoke," consists of paths or ways, practices like physical exercises and breathing control, that help us recognize our identity with God. The physical exercises are the best-known kinds of yoga, but yoga can also be selfless action performed as a duty. The *Upanishads* and the *Vedanta* school of Hindu theology stress the oneness of all reality. Through meditation one can achieve knowledge of oneness with God, and yoga helps one "tune out" distractions in order to concentrate on Brahman.

Many Hindus approach the universal spirit through devotion to a particular incarnation of god. According to texts on Hinduism, Brahman has many *avatara*, or incarnations, including *Devi*, *Siva* (sometimes spelled *Shiva*), and *Vishnu*. Vishnu is the creating and preserving god who maintains the stability of the cosmos. Siva, the creating and destroying god, embodies the opposites of the universe: good and evil, birth and death, female and male. Devi, the goddess and mother of the cosmos, represents the universe's creative energy and power as well as the forces of death and destruction. Devotees of these gods may believe "their" god is more forceful and sublime than another god.

These gods have other gods associated with them as well. Siva is associated with *Ganesa*, the elephant-headed god of wisdom who is Shiva's son. Vishnu has a number of avatars or incarnations. The most notable ones are *Rama* and *Krishna*. Krishna has long been associated with divine love and *bhakti*. In some scriptures he is the blue-skinned and playful god, but in the *Bhagavad-Gita* he provides one of the most profound philosophies by which people have lived. Devi is known through incarnations like *Kali*, *Duga*, *Radha* (the consort of Krishna), *Parvati*, Shiva's wife, and *Lakshmi* (the wife of Vishnu).

Deities are often worshiped in Hindu temples. "Favorite deities are called *ishtadeva*," says Dr. Bhardwaj, "the deity that one has recognized as one's favorite icon. . . . All of these individual deities are worshiped according to the liturgy that has developed over time. In the temples, the deities are worshiped as though they were physically present there. Thus they are roused from sleep and worshiped at that time. All throughout the day they are worshiped as though they were physically there. Flowers are brought to them; food is brought to them at appropriate times during the day. Lamps are lit in their honor. Ultimately at night they are literally put to bed.

"But these are theistic worshipers in the temples. There are many Hindus who do not worship the universal spirit through the icons. They think of God as totally beyond attributes, and so God cannot be encompassed in any one of our adorations or definitions. Because they regard him in that way they regard him as an abstract principle. It is harder to focus upon God in the abstract, but many Hindus prefer that way. . . . Very few people are absolutely fixated upon worshiping the images or worshiping the formless spirit. All of these things together are objects of worship. . . .

Spiritual Types

Hinduism recognizes a fact that many Christians forget or do not realize: everyone has his or her own spiritual type. In other words, we learn faith and grow spiritually in different ways. As presented on page 13, a book that explains this well is Corinne Ware's *Discover Your Spiritual Type*[6], which discusses four broadly defined spiritual types. These types are repeated here:

• "Head" Spirituality. This person thinks through religious ideas and appreciates good sermons, good books, writing, and other activities involving logical thought.

• "Heart" Spirituality. This person experiences spiritual reality in a more emotional way: through such activities as music, testimony, and spontaneous rather than liturgical services.

• "Mystic" Spirituality. This person experiences spiritual reality in nonverbal, contemplative ways: through meditation, intuitive insight into God's reality, or a simple lifestyle.

• "Kingdom" Spirituality. Such a person finds spirituality in action, work, social justice, and striving for a vision.

How do you see the various paths of Hinduism fitting into Ware's scheme? How does the fact that Hinduism recognizes several spiritual paths, without competition among them, help you better appreciate various Christian pathways?

"The Hindu priests are really functionaries, not pastors. One has to recognize the different roles of these people. Hindu worship is an individual commitment to God, and the priest is a functionary who helps focus upon the actual acts of worship. The laity, then, gives direction to local Hinduism."

Some important Hindu worship ceremonies coincide with rites of passage such as birth, a boy's first haircut, a girl's first period, marriage, and so on until death. In temples, representations of the gods are cared for throughout the day. With lay worshipers usually in attendance, priests awaken the gods, give them food, bathe them, and decorate them with flowers. Temples may be very large or comparatively small. Many Hindu homes have shrines to gods. Some shrines, however, are places of pilgrimage. The *Prayaga* shrine at Allahabad at the juncture of the Ganges and Yamuma rivers is a holy site for millions of pilgrims.

Many Paths

Because it is a complex religion with many noncompeting paths within its theological and devotional traditions, Hinduism not surprisingly accepts the views of other faiths. "Hindus recognize that other religions and paths of thought could be as valid as theirs," says Dr. Bhardwaj. "There is no contest. . . . One thing that I find is the idea that reality or truth cannot be the exclusive property of one particular faith. Reality can be explored by various paths. That is one thing that seems to be continuous in Hindu thought. Sometimes, though, it makes it difficult to accommodate with other religions that would make their own path the exclusive path. That makes it difficult—and difficult to understand!"

> **Closing**
> Sing together "Spirit of the Living God" or a similar hymn. Thank God for the things you have learned in these lessons so far. Ask God to help you stay strong as you go through your life's tasks and responsibilities.

Notes

1. Theodore Ludwig, *The Sacred Paths: Understanding the Religions of the World* (New York: Macmillan, 1989), pages 253–59.

2. David R. Kinsley, *Hinduism: A Cultural Perspective* (Englewood Cliffs, NJ: Prentice Hall, 1982), pages 122–31.

3. Ibid., page 89–90.

4. Ludwig, page 298.

5. Mary Pat Fisher, *Living Religions,* 4th edition (Upper Saddle River, NJ: Prentice Hall, 1999), pages 98–102.

6. Corinne Ware, *Discover Your Spiritual Type: A Guide to Individual and Congregational Growth* (Washington, DC, 1995) pages 36–45.

For More Information

Look for books about Hinduism that can help deepen your understanding.

- Gavin Flood, *An Introduction to Hinduism.* Cambridge: Cambridge University Press, 1996.
- David R. Kinsley, *Hindu Goddesses: Visions of the Divine Feminine in the Hindu Religious Tradition.* Berkeley: University of California Press, 1988.
- R. C. Zaehner, *Hinduism.* New York: Oxford University Press, 2nd edition, 1982.

CHAPTER 5
THE PATH TO FREEDOM

Buddhism

**The Problem
of Suffering**

> **Focus**: In this session we examine how Buddhism offers a way to happiness and inner freedom.

Years ago, when I
was growing up in Vandalia, a local minister stood impatiently in a bank line. One of my parents noticed how huffy this preacher had become and thought his impatience was a poor Christian witness. In retrospect, I felt bad for the preacher, since I hate long lines. How many times have I unin-

Gathering

Greet one another. Tell about personal news and events that have occurred since you last met. Ask one another for support and prayers. What makes for true happiness? List your responses.

Prepare an envelope in which you have a coupon for dinner at an area restaurant. Or you may create a coupon for a pie, a loaf of bread, or another baked item that has been prepared ahead. Announce to the group that you will have a drawing for the coupon later in the session. About halfway through the session, have a drawing and give the coupon to the winner. Ask: What feelings would you experience if you won the coupon? if someone else won the coupon? How does the desire for the meal or baked item compare or contrast to the desire for a spiritual benefit?

Pray for an awareness of the ways our desire for material things might affect our desire for spiritual growth and our sense of God's presence. Pray for any needs mentioned at the beginning.

> Brainstorm all the things that come to your mind when you think of Buddha and Buddhists. What about the religion do you not understand? What do you want to know about Buddhism?

tentionally provoked others to question the depth of my religious walk?

Whether the difficulty is a momentary aggravation or very severe suffering, is serenity in the face of difficulty a "proof" of one's faith? If serenity is not a proof of faith, is it at least a demonstration of the seriousness of one's religious journey?

Rather than beginning with conventional religious questions like, "Who is God and how can I know him?" Buddhism starts with the fact of human disquiet and suffering and offers both a diagnosis and a cure. Like Hinduism, Buddhism springs from beliefs in *karma*, *samsara*, and *moksha*. But it has developed into a religion that can be practiced alongside other faiths as well. A friend of mine humorously calls himself a "Zen Methodist."

I quoted Dr. Robert Schwartz, assistant professor of education in the department of counseling at the University of Akron, in Chapter 1. Prof.

> If you were being interviewed as to the essential principles of Christianity, what would you say? Jot down a few ideas. How "useful" are those principles? Are they "generalizable to anybody" or do they apply to certain people? Explain.

Schwartz's background is Jewish, but he has explored the Buddhist tradition for several years. He notes that the Buddhist principles are "generalizable to anybody." As originally conceived, the religion is very practical, he says, because it does not deal with esoteric

teachings or realities taken on faith. "The religion is based on not being selfish and egotistical and self-centered. It's a very hopeful, practical, and usable religion. The religion is not an easy way to follow, but the basic principles are easy to understand."

Siddhartha

Siddhartha Gautama was born about 563 B.C. in the Himalayan foothills. His family was high-caste Hindu, members of the *kshatriya*, the warrior and ruler caste. Much of his life is legendary. According to tradition, his father gave him a life of ease and luxury. The father wanted

Siddhartha to succeed him as ruler rather than to become a religious teacher like a Gautama ancestor.

Siddhartha married and had a son. Although he lived luxuriously with attendants, dancing girls, and finery, Siddhartha questioned the meaning of his life. As the story goes, Siddhartha rode into the countryside on four separate occasions and saw four things that changed the course of his life. One was the sight of an elderly man, whereby he learned of old age. Then he saw a sick person, whereby he learned of disease. Next he saw a dead person, and he learned of life's impermanence. Finally he saw a Hindu *sannyasi*, that is, a man who has given up all possessions; and Siddhartha considered renunciation of the world as a possible religious path to insight. Eventually Siddhartha left his family and wealth. He dressed simply like that world-renouncing holy man and proceeded to discover the truth about life.

At first he tried traditional yogic practices. Later he practiced harsh self-denial. He nearly starved himself and never bathed, punishing his body in order to bring about enlightenment. He achieved some insight but hoped for something greater. While meditating beneath a tree, he experienced a vision of karma and the cycles of rebirth. Finally he understood the reason for suffering in life, as well as the path to happiness. He began to teach the basics of Buddhist doctrine to a group of five followers at a place called Deer Park. Siddhartha died in 483 B.C.

> At what times in your life have you felt like a sincere religious seeker but you could not quite find what you were looking for? Perhaps you did not know what you were looking for until you found it. What was your experience? Was your search solitary, or did it involve others?

The faith spread through India and eventually to China, Tibet, Nepal, Southeast Asia, and Japan. No longer a large religion in India, Buddhism has thrived in other parts of the world. One Buddhist branch, *Theravada*, is strong in Southeast Asia and Sri Lanka. An Indian emperor, Asoka, accepted Buddhism in 297 B.C. and sent missionaries to many countries, helping the faith to spread. Consequently, the branch called *Mahayana* took on many qualities of faiths around Asia. Among the Buddhist scriptures the *Tipitaka* (Three Baskets) are important to the Theravada tradition, while Mahayana Buddhists add *sutras*, which means "scriptures," to the original collection of sacred writings.

The two branches take different approaches to the teachings of Siddhartha, which were not written and compiled until the first century

Koans

Zen koans are statements intended to snap us out of our usual ways of looking at things. A famous koan is "What is the sound of one hand clapping?" D. T. Suzuki gives two others[1]:

"What is your original face before you were born?"

"The cypress-tree in the courtyard" (in answer to the question, "What is the ultimate principle of Buddhism?").

In focusing upon the koan we are supposed to get beyond the usual cognitive and verbal ways of understanding in order to experience truth intuitively.

Christian evangelists speak of "praying through" or breaking through our mental barriers to experience Christ. Can you think of other analogies in Christianity to the koan?

B.C. Theravada approaches Buddhism as a set of philosophical and psychological teachings and practices. Mahayana incorporates more "religious" tenets such as enlightened beings, called *bodhisattvas*, and prayers. Mahayanist sects include Pure Land, which emphasizes the god Amitabha, who brings the faithful to a lovely afterlife. Zen, another Mahayana branch, aims at insight, knowledge gained through meditation, riddles called *koan*, and even startling students to enlightenment. Still another branch, *Nichiren Shoshu*, emphasizes a particular scripture, the *Lotus Sutra*, as key to the truth. Tibetan Buddhism is related to Mahayana but is categorized by a separate name, *Vajrayana*. Tibetan Buddhism is a complex sect that uses formulas, manuals called *tantras*, and prayer wheels. All these Buddhist forms aim at the same insight-experience: overcoming suffering through *nirvana*.

Four Truths and a Path

The word *Buddha* means one who is enlightened, or one who has awakened to the truth. Siddhartha the Buddha taught "the four noble truths" that formed the basis of Buddhist doctrine.[2]

How do you understand selfishness? self-centeredness? How do you understand self-esteem? What differences do you see between the concepts? What makes the difference between one who is self-centered and one who is altruistic?

1. *Life is dukkha. Dukkha* means suffering. Although we do not necessarily suffer every minute of our lives, we do experience degrees of

suffering at various times. We become sick. We experience disappointments. We want that which we cannot have. We are dissatisfied.

Read Luke 10:27. How does Jesus' teaching about love of God, neighbor, and self compare and contrast with the four noble truths of Buddhism?

Eventually someone we love dies. Eventually we die, too. Life is imperfect, dislocated. Life does not meet our expectations.

2. *Suffering is caused by desire.* "Desire" is not simply a longing for someone or something. Desire is also our expectations. If life were fair, we would not be trapped by disease. We would not be trapped in situations over which we have no control. We would get that which we desire: love, health, money, well-being, and so on. Sometimes we get these things, sometimes we do not. When we do not, we inevitably suffer. Those expectations imply a certain amount of self-centeredness; life does not live up to *my* expectations, and that disappointment in turn increases suffering.

3. *In order to end suffering, end desire.* If we can extinguish our desires and the concomitant self-centeredness, we can end suffering. We need to reach a state in which we are free of self-centeredness, expectations, and desire. We will not suddenly become freed from all disappointment, pain, death, and so on; but we will have a very high degree of inner freedom in spite of circumstances.

4. *To end desire, we must follow the Eightfold Path.* The Eightfold Path is a disci-

The Eightfold Path[3]

1. **Right understanding** means understanding reality via the Four Noble Truths.
2. **Right thought** means dealing with our emotional "baggage" and bringing our inner self into peace and harmony.
3. **Right speech** means getting rid of foolish conversation, gossiping, lying, swearing, and replacing such things with positive talk.
4. **Right action** means doing good and avoiding evil.
5. **Right livelihood** means avoiding those occupations that hurt and exploit other people.
6. **Right effort** means working toward the goal of inner harmony, understanding that the way may not be easy.
7. **Right mindfulness** means developing the mind to reach liberation.
8. **Right meditation** means developing practices that calm the mind.

plined set of practices aimed at achieving inner freedom. In Buddhist teaching, the Eightfold Path helps you reach *nirvana,* or that state wherein you are above suffering. Nirvana is both a mental and a spiritual state in which you have not only curbed but also eliminated attachment, so that happiness and compassion rule your mind. Nirvana happens as a moment of insight and realization, an "ah ha!" experience. *Attachment,* in turn, means basing your whole happiness upon something that does not last (and nothing in life lasts!), or being so psychologically "hung up" on some thing or situation that it causes or perpetuates suffering in your life.

> Find a partner and talk about: (1) an experience of being somewhere or in some situation in which you did not want to be (illness, a bad job, an unhappy marriage), (2) an experience of deeply wanting something you could not have (an unrequited love situation, some possession that was beyond your means). How did you deal with these situations? How did God help you in these situations? Do you feel like you were calm and accepting, or upset and chagrined? What connections do you make between these experiences and the noble truths of Buddhism?

As we sat in a noisy, busy student union that contrasted with the peacefulness of our subject, I asked Prof. Schwartz to talk about the noble truths. "In Western society," he said, "people spend a lot of money on technology to escape pain. Pain is not necessarily a bad thing; it's just reality. But it is possible to reduce and in fact eliminate suffering in this lifetime, and that's what [Buddhists] speak about when they speak of 'nirvana.' Nirvana means becoming enlightened to the point that you're above the world of pain.

"There is a path that can take you there. The path curbs attachment and desire and also eliminates aversion or hatred, which is the opposite side of the same thing. If you look at what causes pain or suffering, it's very, very difficult to think of any instance that is not your craving or desiring something you can't have, or your hating something that you do have. Basically everything falls into those categories. People's ignorance of this fact often keeps them in a continuous cycle of suffering."

Since the Buddhist worldview springs from Hindu roots, I also asked Prof. Schwartz to discuss *karma* as it relates to Buddhism. "You cannot change the past, but you can influence the future," he told me. "The word *karma* means action. It's what you do now that affects your life in the future. A person in a Buddhist country might say it affects your future lives, not just your life in the future. But even if you take reincarnation out of the picture, it makes a lot of sense. What you say and do and even what you think, has a ripple effect. Quantum physics has proved what is called the butterfly effect. At a microscopic level, the flapping of a butterfly's wings, in Miami, Florida, where I'm from, has a ripple effect that changes the climate in Alaska, or even in Tibet. Every single thing is that interrelated, even at a microscopic level. Karma has even more of an impact than that, because it mostly refers to your direct interactions with other people." He notes that you can have a positive impact on persons by verbalizing appreciation, doing them a favor, and helping them. You can also have a negative impact on persons by speaking negatively, criticizing their work, and thinking pessimistically. Either way, says Prof. Schwartz, "you change their emotional state," in an analogous manner to the way a butterfly's wings have a long-range effect. "You change how they relate to the next person they come in contact with. It has a ripple effect everywhere. That's karma! If you're calm and aware and try to affect another person's happiness, you affect your own future."

> What experiences have you had in which another person's or group's actions affected you for better or for worse? What happened? Were you a participant or an observer in the situation? When have your actions, either good or bad, significantly affected others? What did you learn, if anything, from the experiences?

> What is something, or someone, in your life that you would never want to do without? What would you do if you no longer had that thing or that person in your life? What is it like to lose something very precious to you? How might the Buddhist idea of attachment be useful in handling the feelings of loss?

Thus, in Buddhism, sin does not consist of bad choices, bad actions, and the forgetfulness of God. Sin, to use that "Western" term, is the self-centeredness that causes one to cling to the phenomenal world of suffering and selfishness. Redemption comes from the insights, and the resulting actions, that come from one's realiza-

> Have you ever attended a church with a low degree of joy and interpersonal caring? a church with a high degree of those qualities? What made the difference?

Rank these things according to how much they give you a sense of inner peace and self-worth. Omit ones that do not apply to you.

- My vehicle
- My parents
- God's love for me
- My income/savings accounts
- My spouse
- My children
- My collection of _____.
- My service to others
- My education
- My friendships
- My prestige and reputation
- My job
- People's approval
- My looks
- My house and lawn or garden
- My membership in organizations

What other things can you think of?

tion of the noble truths. Sin is attachment while freedom is nonattachment. Since Prof. Schwartz is a counselor, I asked him how attachment and nonattachment figure into people's inner perspectives.

Prof. Schwartz acknowledged that we live in a society that reinforces the idea that personal worth depends upon productivity, possessions, and prestige. Such attachments recreate one's identity. Prof. Schwarz says that when he goes to places like Nepal or Thailand, he notices how free the people are, even though they have so little compared to what we have. "There's a word in Thai, *sanook*, that's roughly translated 'having fun,' " he said. "Everything they do is *sanook*. If you go to a bank, the workers there are likely to be laughing and joking around. If a teller drops some coins, they all laugh and say, 'Oh, what happened, you drank too much last night.' It's all having fun and not being stressed out. It's living in the moment. It's just an exhilarating thing to see. I think it's all because Buddhism is part of the culture, so they're all in touch with each other and care about each other. They care more about living beings than things."

Interrelatedness and Compassion

Prof. Schwartz observes that different schools of Buddhism offer the same core values and meanings in a similar way that different branches of Christianity offer them. "You should live a life as fully as possible with compassion and love for all beings, with love and kindness, gentleness, patience, tolerance, and most of all sensitivity to, as they say, all sentient beings. That means any being that has any amount of consciousness. When Tibetan monks build a new temple they dig down into the soil

> Do you feel much connection with the nonhuman world? Do you or anyone you know like to go hunting? How does the idea of noninjury to the animal and insect world seem to you?

carefully so as not to hurt the worm and they replant the worm. Western science is just starting to prove that every living being has emotions and feels pain. A major Buddhist goal is to try to your utmost not to cause pain in another living being and if possible to improve their happiness. So it's important to have a high degree of sensitivity to that, every day."

Prof. Schwartz believes the value of compassion is part of the identity of Buddhists. "They're much less aggressive, much less competitive. That struck me when I returned to America from Thailand three weeks ago. Westerners are very success-oriented. Americans spend so much time and energy trying to gain money, power, prestige, and control. In Buddhist philosophy, everything is interrelated—we're all one, and we're all part of the universe. There is no duality. There is no 'me and you and him and her.' People don't say, 'This is mine; don't touch it.' 'This is yours; so don't let it in my personal space.' "

Prof. Schwartz sees that excessive involvement with ego or self leads to the need to control. "We have such a strong desire to hold on and control things. It dominates our lives." He believes that we put so much time and energy into it that we become competitive, sometimes aggressive, and ultimately isolated from other people. "You can't simultaneously be one with others and connected with others and also control your own space and boundaries, focused on gaining something for yourself."

Contemporary lifestyle conveniences that are intended to make our lives easier actually isolate us from one another. "We have fast food, prescription medicines we obtain through the drive-through, computers, and e-mail. We don't have to talk on the phone anymore, let alone see someone in person. Everything is quicker and easier." Schwartz sees that these conveniences increase our need for instant gratification. "We want everything now and we become very intolerant and impatient, especially when we want something, let alone when we can't get something immediately."

> Two very famous Christian Scripture passages are John 15:11 and Philippians 4:7. What are the sources of a Christian's peace and joy? How do you cultivate peace and joy? How might prayer or meditation help you cultivate them?

Meditation

Following Buddhist teaching, Schwartz believes we can become more tolerant, patient, and compassionate through meditation. One Buddhist kind of meditation is *vipassana*, wherein one calms the mind by first concentrating upon one's breathing. Vipassana also includes "walking meditation," during which one concentrates on the movements of one's body. *Zazen* is another kind of meditation wherein one sits in a prescribed posture for a period of time in order to calm the mind and make the mind open to insight. Calmness and focus are important, Prof. Schwartz says, "so you can look deeply within yourself, into the reality of life, in order to understand and make it conscious for you. It's one thing to get a glimpse of the truth and another thing to let it into your life. For me it's very important, to be calm, physiologically, and to take a step outside the interpersonal 'stuff' that can keep you bogged down and can lead to suffering."

God

Where is God in all this? I told Prof. Schwartz that, as I saw it, Siddhartha emphasized the path over an idea of God. "Absolutely," he said. "Most Buddhists view the world without one all-powerful being who is the best or the only one. It goes back to the oneness of all things. We all have personal power and the ability to help one another. We don't have to claim something as the best or the only one, even if it is God. Belief in God can be another form of attachment. The stronger the attachment, the more problems arise. And, yes, even God falls into that category. It's clinging to an idea to the point you harm and may even kill other human beings. Usually we put material things above life, but ideas are the same way. Ideas can become reified

> What is your response to the statement that we do not have to claim something as the best or the only one, even if it is God, because that's another form of attachment? How does this view compare with a Christian view of God?

and take on a life of their own; and we have the potential to put them above life as well, because we personalize those ideas and think of them as 'ours.' "

Buddhist Views of an Afterlife

I asked Prof. Schwartz about the Buddhist concept of afterlife. He e-mailed me: "Paul, all forms of Buddhism that I'm aware of, which is not all of them, believe in the 'afterlife,' or more accurately reincarnation and enlightenment. But there is no 'heaven' per se. When you die your consciousness enters the universal consciousness/energy, and if you haven't attained enlightenment (nirvana) you are reincarnated back into the world of samsara (suffering). The difference between schools of Buddhism has more to do with one's ultimate goal. In Theravada Buddhism personal nirvana/liberation is the goal, but in Mahayana Buddhism . . . the goal is to be enlightened but still to come back to earth to help others attain enlightenment. This person is called a *Bodhisattva*. The Dalai Lama is the 'Bodhisattva of Compassion' because he keeps 'coming back' in human form to help others reach enlightenment."

Clearly, Buddhism would tend to be very noncompetitive toward other faiths. One might say that, instead of offering doctrinal truth, it offers practical truth: a path to freedom and compassionate living.

"If you throw a stone into a lake," Prof. Schwartz told me, "the first thing you'll notice is that the ripples go outward. But the second thing that happens is, when they hit the shore, they come back in toward the center, toward you. So karma affects your own life. In Thai there's a famous saying that they live by, *tom dee, dai dee*, 'if you do good, you'll get good.' And that's karma!"

> **Closing**
> Many people are familiar with the "serenity prayer." What are the similarities and differences you see between Buddhist teachings of nirvana and nonattachment and this prayer? To conclude this lesson, pray together, "God grant me the serenity to accept the things I cannot change, the courage to change the things I can, and the wisdom to know the difference."

Notes

1. D. T. Suzuki, *An Introduction to Zen Buddhism* (New York: Grove Press, 1964), pages 104, 106.

2. Theodore M. Ludwig, *The Sacred Path: Understanding the Religions of the World* (New York: Macmillan, 1989), pages 307, 323.

3. Mary Pat Fisher, *Living Religions,* 4th edition (Upper Saddle River, New Jersey: Prentice Hall, 1999), pages 145–46.

For More Information

Find some good books about Buddhism such as

• D. T. Suzuki, *An Introduction to Zen Buddhism.* New York: Grove Press, 1964.

• The Dalai Lama, *The Art of Happiness.* New York: Riverhead Books, 1998.

• Edward Cronze, *Buddhism: Its Essence and Development.* New York: Harper & Row, 1975.

• Thich Nhat Hanh, *Peace Is Every Step: The Path of Mindfulness in Everyday Life.* New York: Bantam Books, 1991.

• Thich Nhat Hanh, *Being Peace.* Berkeley, CA: Parallax Press, 1996 (reprint edition).

CHAPTER 6
KNOWING ONE GOD

Sikhism and Baha'i

Two Widespread Faiths

Focus: This lesson explores two worldwide faiths that emerged from the Muslim world.

In this chapter, we look at two of the newest major religions of the world: Sikhism and Baha'i. Both arose in a Muslim context, and both faiths are very widespread throughout the world. Yet they are different and did not influence each other. Sikhism has fifteenth-century roots in the Punjab region of India, while Baha'i emerged from Persia during the nineteenth century. As you read this lesson, think about the different ways these two faiths emphasize oneness.

Gathering

Greet one another and welcome any newcomers. Provide quick updates on life since the last time you met. Read together Jesus' "unity" prayer for his disciples, John 17:20-26. What is the unity for which Christ asks? What are the signs of unity among Jesus' followers? Do Christians display this kind of unity?

Sikhism: "There Is Only God, Which Is God"

Hinduism and Islam seem incompatible as religious tradi-

List a few things you know about Sikhism. Are there any Sikh congregations in your area? Check out websites, *www.sikhnet.com*, and *www.sikh.net* for more information.

tions, but in areas of what is now northern India, people have been enriched by both. A Muslim-born poet named Kabir (1440–1518) hoped to unite elements of the two faiths by stressing one God who, through love, can free a person from the cycles of *samsara*. Kabir departed from the *Vedas* and de-emphasized traditional Hindu worship practices. Kabir, whom a few Indians still follow, is still honored by Sikhs.

Nanak (1469–1538) was, like Siddhartha centuries before, a Hindu of the Kshatriya caste. Living in an area where Hindus and Muslims lived, Nanak was exposed to both traditions from an early time. Like Siddhartha and Jesus, he was about thirty when he became a religious teacher. Nanak received a vision of God as he walked through a forest. "There is neither Hindu nor Mussulman [Muslim]," he declared, "so whose path shall I follow? I shall follow God's path."[1]

As a guru (teacher), Nanak traveled throughout India and, traditionally, even to Arabia where he visited the Muslim holy sites

Followers of his teachings were called by the Punjabi word *Sikh*, or "disciples." When he was fifty-two, he and his family moved to Karatarpur, where many of his followers lived. For the remaining seventeen years of his life he taught the basic principles he received from God. Following his death a succession of gurus continued those principles. The third guru collected the faith's scriptures, the *Adi Granth* ("original collection"), which eventually became an authoritative edition. The fourth guru established the Sikh center of worship, the Golden Temple at the town of Amritsar.

By the beginning of the next century, the 1600s, Sikhs began to be persecuted and two gurus were martyred during the seventeenth century. To denote membership in the military order (the *Khalsa*) established by the tenth and last guru, Sikh men were obligated to keep their hair uncut and to wear it beneath a turban, as well as to carry a dagger and other tokens. Some Sikh sects do not follow the military aspects.

After many years of struggle the Sikhs founded a kingdom in

The Punjab

Check the Internet or an encyclopedia for information about the Punjab, a territory that was divided when the borders of India and Pakistan were established in 1947. Since Pakistan was predominantly Muslim, two million Sikhs emigrated, many to India and others to other parts of the world. What is some of the history of Sikhs and Hindus since 1947?

the Punjab region during the late eighteenth and early nineteenth centuries. The British annexed this region in 1849; but when the British left with Indian independence in 1947, they did not reestablish the Punjab kingdom. The Indian government set up a Sikh state in Punjab in 1966, but Sikhs still dream of greater autonomy from India for that region. About seventeen million Sikhs live in the world today.

Visiting a Congregation

Sikh worship happens in a *gurdwara*, a public worship house. One Sunday morning I drove about ten miles from my home to the Guru Nanak Foundation in Richfield, Ohio. I had been told that, if I came at eleven in the morning, I could find someone to talk to about my project. The worship service was drawing to a close. Inside, people had their shoes off and all the men's hair was covered. I asked if I should remove my shoes. I did and also covered my hair with a square of cloth. Shortly Ratanjit S. Sondhe, CEO of the Poly-Carb chemical corporation of Cleveland, Ohio, greeted me warmly and, with a happy group of his friends, told me about the faith.

> What elements of dress, if any, are important in your worship? What aspects of dress in worship give you a sense of awe or respect for God?
>
> How does dress vary in different congregations or in different types of Christian worship experiences?

Sikh Beliefs

"Sikh is the fifth largest religion in the world," Mr. Sondhe said "The founder's name was Guru Nanak. At this point in time, we do not have a live guru. All the gurus have given us poetry, which we call *Gurbani*; that has become part of *Guru Granth Sahib*. That is our religious scripture, which we consider a guru, as well. *Guru* in the Indian language means a guide, teacher, and prophet: all those things combined. The feeling for guru is so strong, that once somebody asked, if God and the guru are standing before you, whose feet would you touch first? Only through the guru do I reach God."

The scripture I referred to earlier, the *Adi Granth*, is another name for

> Given the choice, do you prefer prose or poetry in your devotions? How often do you turn to the Psalms? Do you ever read hymns from your hymnal—either to sing or to read for spiritual insight? Write a hymn of your own. If you are not poetically inclined, write ideas of what you would include in your hymn.

the *Guru Granth Sahib*. It includes hymns by Nanak and his immediate successor, Guru Angad, as well as hymns by Kabir and others. The scripture contains nearly 3,400 hymns in all. "In the scripture," says Mr. Sondhe, "not only do we have poetry from our ten gurus, but also contributions made by thirty-six non-Sikh saints. Some of them were from different religions like Hindu, Muslim, Christianity; and some of them were from a different time as the gurus. But the most amazing part is that their thought processes are absolutely identical."

As the Sikh scripture contains hymns from different religious backgrounds, Sikhism itself recognizes different religions. "If I understood what is in *Gurbani,* which is *Granth Sahib*," said Mr. Sondhe, "if I then want to

> What attracts you most to a person's religious faith: a verbal appeal, a positive personal example, or a combination of the two?

follow the typical religion like Christianity or Hinduism, I can practice that religion much better, because the *Gurbani* cleanses you and prepares you to follow any path you want to follow. So in that sense Sikhism really is a universal religion." Mr. Sondhe noted that several persons worshiping that morning were members of other religions. Sikhism is not a faith that tries to convert others nor seeks to be the sole religious path. Since the early days people came to the faith through the example of Sikhs' discipline and service.

Mr. Sondhe continued, "Our scripture starts with a word, *Ik Onkar.* That is the key to the entire understanding of the *Gurbani*. If you miss the

> Read the familiar 1 Corinthians 12. What is the basis for unity among Christians? How does the passage compare or contrast to the concept of *Ik Onkaar?*

meaning of that word, you're going to be following the rituals but not the sense of the faith. If you followed and understood the meaning of that word, the rest of it falls into place. *Ik Onkar* [sometimes spelled *Ik Onkaar*] means, 'there is only one.' There are not two. That one, is God. Once I understand that, you and I are not two. Just like I have two hands and two legs, my leg is not the same as my hand but they are one, a part of this body. If someone cuts off my hand, it is no longer part of the body; it cannot function. If we are an extension of that ultimate God, and that's all we are, so our purpose in life becomes very clear to us: to serve that greater body."

The oneness of God has implications for us, both in terms of our proper self-understanding and our responsibilities for service. "In our scripture," said Mr. Sondhe, "there is a constant stress. Find out who you are. Until you find out who you are, every calculation you'll make will be

> Have you ever been called upon to render some menial service, either for your church or to help someone? What did you have to do? Did you feel you gave glory to God? If not, what would have made the task more like true service?

wrong. Who are you? You are a man or a woman, old or young. But these are all the qualities of your human body, not you. The 'I' is not a separate entity. Once you understand that, your thought process of 'I, me, and mine' stems from your basic ignorance of understanding. This human body, this instrument, is given to you to serve and to love. That is the sense of *Gurbani;* that is the sense of Sikhism. Our whole purpose, our very existence, is to serve the human race."

Sikhism thus aims at love and service. No distinctions exist in Sikh worship, an important thing for instance in India where castes have separated people. Worshipers are not divided by gender or class or ethnic background. In the *gurdwara*, a common meal called the *langar* is provided to anyone who wishes to participate. In daily prayers, God's name is repeated over and over to help one receive blessing, aid, and inner strength. Sikhs give a tenth of their income and emphasize service, even very menial service.

> Think about the Sikh "uniform," and read Ephesians 6:10-17. What signs do you give to the world concerning your own spiritual disciplines and allegiances? Although the author of Ephesians is speaking metaphorically, what are some situations wherein you see fighting as an act of faith?

As noted above, Sikhism has had a military component, as a form of service that protects people's freedom of worship and religion. Mr. Sondhe, wearing a turban like the other men of the congregation, explained. "Three hundred years back, there was a Muslim ruler in India, Aurangzeb, who was like bin Laden; he wanted to convert every religion into Muslim. In northern India, at that point, they donated their oldest sons to become Sikhs, in this particular uniform, to protect the nation. That is why this uniform evolved. If I joined the armed forces or police force, my purpose is to protect and serve society. This is the uniform that reminds me, that this [human body] is just the outer shell."

> **Dualism**
>
> Many Christians think of the universe as created by but separated from God; God is present with us spiritually, not as a part of things. The things around us are not God. This way of thinking is called "dualism." The spiritual and material are two separate but related things. What do you see as the basis for service to and responsibility for other people in a dualistic Christian perspective?

When you recognize that your true self is not your human body, you understand your role in life. "The real 'I' that resides in me is the divine extension in me of the divine," Mr. Sondhe noted, "and basically my role here is to serve the divine within every living person. The word *Sikh* also translates into 'student.' In order for me to carry out my mission to serve the human race, I have to place myself in the student mode. So I'm constantly upgrading my skills and understanding so I can serve the human race better. That is the essence of the Sikh philosophy."

It has often been said that Sikhism combines aspects of Hinduism and Islam. Like Islam, it stresses God's oneness; and like Hinduism it teaches the reality of karma and cycles of reincarnation in the afterlife. I mentioned that Sikhs believe in one God, and Mr. Sondhe corrected, "A lot of people translate that as 'only one God.' It should be: 'There is only One, which is God.' There are not two. All our problems in society are from that basic miscalculation that there are two. We segregate ourselves in many ways. But we are really one. Our cells exist to serve our body. They sacrifice their very existence. But every once in a while a cell emerges that serves itself, even at the expense of the body. We call it a cancer cell. That clearly tells us that the moment I as a human being have my own agenda and am self-serving at the expense of our society, then I've become a cancer cell."

In order to be a healthy, rather than "cancerous" member of society, one

74

must learn to serve others. Thus the ethical orientation of Sikhism is toward service, but also toward "adding value" to the world. Mr. Sondhe says that the ethical thrust of Sikhism is not really "how to

> What about the Sikh faith sounds very similar and compatible to your beliefs? What sounds different?

become a good person. The question really is to understand the psychology of the universe. The question is, how can I add value? If you are serving a customer, rather thinking, 'How can I sell him something?' now you can ask, 'How can I add value to him?' I am in the listening mode and try to find out 'What does he need?' Then I come around and serve that. Everywhere you see success happening, it has this ingredient present."

A quotation from the Tenth Guru, Guru Gobind Singh, seems apropos:

Same are the temple and the mosque
And same are the forms of worship therein.
All human beings are one though apparently many,
Realize, therefore, the essential unity of mankind.[2]

Baha'i: Sun Shining in a Mirror

A New, Yet Ancient Faith

My introduction to Baha'i was the musical duo Seals and Crofts, whom I first heard on 1970s AM radio when I was in high school. I then read an article about them in one of my rock and roll magazines. I remember too thinking that Baha'i principles seemed very lovely.

> What do you know about Baha'i? Among other sites, *www.us.bahai.com* provides background on the Bab and Baha'u'llah as well as other aspects of the faith's history. Check out the Web site. What do you learn from the information there?

Baha'i is the newest major faith in the world. About six million people in over 300 countries worldwide profess to the Baha'i faith. Although Baha'i is much smaller in numbers, the faith is second only to Christianity in worldwide distribution. About 140,000 Baha'is live in the United States.

Baha'i began in the mid-nineteenth century in Iran, then called Persia, where Shi'a Islam is the dominant religion. Shi'ites honor the prophet

What do you think of when you think of Shi'ites? Iran, the Iran hostage crisis of 1979–1981, and other things might come to mind. Study more about their belief in the twelfth imam. Why do you think it is important for some religions to express hope in a future leader to come? Christians believe, for instance, in Jesus' second coming. How does that belief function in your faith?

Muhammad's family as the rightful heirs to his authority. "Twelver" Shi'ites believe that the twelfth successor (*imam*), who disappeared during the 800s, will return someday as the leader of God's people.

In 1844, a Persian man named Mirza Ali Muhammad (1809–1850) announced that he was the new successor to the Prophet. *Mirza* is a title of respect. He called himself the *Bab*, which means "gate," that is, the gate of faith. He taught new revelations from God, set about reforming Muslim practices, and taught the coming unity of all religions. A new, yet greater prophet, he said, would shortly appear, who would set up God's kingdom. He gathered a large number of disciples called the *Babi*. (The "i" ending means "follower of.") But because his teachings aimed at reforming Muslim law, and because his teachings were said to supersede even the

Some religions have beliefs in persons who "open the gate" to faith. Many Buddhists believe in bodhisattvas, or "saints," who help persons reach nirvana. Roman Catholic Christians have saints who intercede for people. What is the difference between a "gate" and the destination itself? What does the door of your house look like? Is it inviting? Do you have a welcome mat? a "no solicitors" sign? a Christian symbol of some sort? What does the image of a door or a gate say to you about faith?

Qur'an, the Persian leadership cracked down on the Babi. Many were executed or imprisoned; the Bab himself met his death by a firing squad in 1850.

The Bab's message spread, however. Several years later, a devoted Babi named Mirza Husayn Ali (1817–1892), who had faced incarceration and torture then finally exile for his beliefs, had a revelation that he was himself the promised, greater prophet. Called Baha'u'llah, which means "the splendor of God" or "the glory of God," Babis followed him during the course of his subsequent ministry. Both the Bab and Baha'u'llah are descendants of Abraham. Baha'u'llah's revelations, books, and writings joined the works of the Bab as Baha'i scripture. The word *Baha'i* means "glory" or "splendor" and became the new name of the earlier Babis.

Following Baha'u'llah's death in 1892, he was succeeded by his son Abbas Effendi, called Abdul Baha, the servant of Baha. After his death in 1921, his eldest nephew, Shoghi Effendi, continued the leadership until he died in 1957. These relatives were not Manifestations of God, a term explained below. Abdul Baha taught the Baha'i faith, traveling through North America and Europe. Shoghi Effendi translated the scriptures and established assemblies. Following his death, Baha'i has been governed by an elected leadership. Although the faith has no "church" or rituals or priests, it has elected groups called assemblies and a worldwide administration. The US national assembly is headquartered in Wilmette, Illinois, and the faith's world center is located in Israel at Mount Carmel.

Religious Neighbors

When I first moved to northeastern Ohio, I noticed a sign along Interstate 76, one of those signs noting that an organization had "adopted" a segment of highway to keep it clean. The local Baha'i community had adopted that particular stretch. The segment was indeed clean! Thus discovering that Baha'is live in the area, I sought a person who could help my project and discovered Jim Geisey, recently retired from Rotek Incorporated as a design engineer, who is part of the Kent State University's campus ministries. We chatted, primarily by e-mail, as he answered my several questions about his faith.

God

What do Baha'is believe about God? Mr. Geisey explained that God, who transcends the universe, is the creator and sustainer of all things. Because God is transcendent, one cannot know God directly. The essence of God is unknowable, even through prayer and meditation. Nevertheless, God's blessings and qualities are known through the Manifestations.

How do you think about doctrines such as the Trinity or the Incarnation? Do you think these are mysteries that we cannot really describe adequately in words, or do you think doctrines quite adequately express the nature of God, Jesus, and the Holy Spirit? Explain. How do they compare with the idea of Manifestations? (See definition of Manifestations on page 78.)

> Which statement below best describes what you might think when you look in a mirror?
>
> • I look pretty good!
> • I wish I hadn't _____.
> • When did I get this old?
> • Am I always this grouchy looking?
> • Hey, I earned these wrinkles!
>
> Do you think mirrors (1) reflect the whole truth, (2) only show the outside, (3) can be deceiving, (4) other?

"The knowledge of God's Manifestations is the knowledge of God," said Mr. Geisey, since God's goodness and glory are made apparent in the Manifestations. "Baha'is often use the analogy of the sun shining in a mirror. In a mirror one can see, not the sun itself, but the reflection of the sun." Similarly, "these Manifestations are like mirrors and reflect the divine attributes of God, but are not God."

What are "Manifestations"? They are the prophets who have come to educate people in different times and cultures. "All major religions" says Mr. Geisey, "are one in essence. We believe any of these are the path to God." As God is a unity, so are his prophets. Baha'is consider Abraham, Buddha, Krishna, Moses, Zoroaster, Jesus, Muhammad, the Bab, and Baha'u'llah as God's Manifestations. "Although their laws differ according to the needs of particular times, their message is basically one." Similarly, the different scriptures of these religions are of divine origin for the benefit of people in different times and places. The purpose of God's Manifestations and scriptures is the same: that people might reach God and gain his blessedness following death.

Religious differences, and with them wars and prejudice, arose in time but did not come from God's Manifestations. Thus Baha'is look to a time when these doctrinal and ritual differences will fall away so that God's basic truths can stand alone.

The unity of God and his prophets implies the unity of all persons. As reflected in Baha'u'llah's own magnanimous and sacrificial attitude toward his persecutors, Baha'is teach harmony among persons. The faith teaches human oneness, universal peace, equality of women and men, and end to prejudice. Compulsory education for all, a common international language, redistribution of wealth in order to end poverty, the harmony of science and religion—these and other principles are core values of Baha'i.

These principles, as well as others explained in the scriptures as well as by Abdul Baha in his speeches during his 1912 US visit, include a high degree of individual willingness to forgive and to seek God's help. "We should all forgive our enemies as well as our friends," Mr. Geisey told me. "We ask God for forgiveness, and we also ask forgiveness for those we've harmed." He added that souls make further progress after death, and people still on earth can pray for them,

> What makes forgiveness easy or difficult for you? How do the Baha'i and Christian ideas about forgiveness compare? Do you think people can be prayed for after their death? Why or why not?

since this world and the spiritual world are connected. Similarly, though we pray to God, we can ask the Manifestations to intercede for us.

Sin and Evil

What is sin and evil according to Baha'i teaching? God's creation is good, and "sin is the absence of God," says Mr. Geisey. Thus "evil is not a reality as such but is a construct that depicts things and actions other than God and his will." When we hold on to human constructs such as class, race, gender, and others, we stress divisions among people rather than concentrating upon our true self, which is our spiritual nature. In turn, we sin when we act according to our human constructs—and thus according to our ignorance of God—instead of recognizing our true natures and God's will for us. "All of the

> What is your "real" self? Make a list of all your qualities, especially the contradictory ones. What connections do you make between these qualities and a "real self"? What differences do you see between the Sikh idea of the "real self" and that of Baha'i? How do these ideas about "real self" compare and contrast with Christian ideas?

Prophets have admonished us to 'know thyself,' " he says. "If we all truly believed that we are all children of God, I think our behavior would change according to God's will. We would have greater respect for each other," notes Mr. Geisey. For instance, Baha'u'llah taught that one of the greatest sins is gossip and backbiting.

As I stated earlier, Baha'i has no "church." Reflecting the faith's insistence on unity and equality, there is no priesthood. Believers worship, however, and show their faith in their everyday lives. "We pray, meditate, fast, serve others, and work in professions that better humankind as means to approach God," said Mr. Geisey. "We are not to become ascetics. . . . Baha'is hold worship services called Feasts every nineteen days. The Feast is threefold in purpose. First is the devotional or to pray and to reflect on the lives and writings of the Manifestations. Second is the fellowship. Third is a communal reflection and consultation about concerns within the community and about our growth as a community."

Baha'is use the word *community* rather than *congregation*. Communities elect their administrative leadership. "In communities where the number is nine or greater, Spiritual Assemblies consisting of nine members are elected by the community to serve as administrative leaders for the year. Once a year we elect a national representative from our district, who will then join others to elect a National Spiritual Assembly also consisting of nine members. The assembly in turn gives us guidance and direction addressing our national concerns." National assemblies around the world elect nine members to the Universal House of Justice that provides guidance and direction for the faith and its ministries around the world.

Afterlife

As far as the afterlife is concerned, Baha'is do not believe in literal places of blessedness or torment or in a personal devil. Thus, as we saw earlier, evil is not a "thing" but is an absence of good. A similar view was held by certain Christian theologians such as St. Augustine. As the author Lewis Hopfe writes, "Baha'i believes that heaven and hell are not places but conditions of the soul. The soul, which is the reality of humankind, is eternal and in continuous progress. When the soul is near to God and God's purposes, that is heaven; when the soul is distant from God, that is hell."[3]

What common aspects do you see between Baha'i and Christianity? What is your reaction to the Baha'i explanation of different religions?

The principles of Baha'i stress unity and the oneness of all people under God. Mr. Geisey quoted the Bab, "We all come from God, and unto Him do we return."

Closing

Think about things that divide religious people. They may be insidious things, like racial prejudice or sexism, or they may be "acceptable" things, like different practices regarding baptism or the appointment of clergy. How important are these things? If you ruled the world, what would you do to eliminate divisions among religious people? What would you do to make people accept your decisions?

Read again John 17:21-23, wherein Jesus prays for the unity of his followers. Pray together for a sense of greater unity among persons, the kind of unity that witnesses to God.

Notes

1. Quoted in Theodore M. Ludwig, *The Sacred Paths: Understanding the Religions of the World* (New York: Macmillan, 1989), page 364.

2. Quoted in Mary Pat Fisher, *Living Religions,* 5th edition (Upper Saddle River, NJ: Prentice Hall, 2002), page 413.

3. Lewis M. Hopfe, *Religions of the World,* 5th edition (New York: Macmillan, 1991), page 447.

For More Information

Sikhism
• For an in-depth look at Sikh scriptures see Manmohan Singh (translator), *Sri Guru Granth Sahib,* 8 volumes, Amritsar: Shronmani Gurdwara Parbandhak Committee, 1962, or Trilochan Singh, et al. (translators), *The Sacred Writings of the Sikhs* (New York: Samuel Weiser, 1973, 1986).
• W. Owen Cole and Piara Singh Sambhi, *The Sikhs: Their Religious Beliefs and Practices* (Sussex, England: Academic Press, 1995).

Baha'i
• William S. Hatcher and J. Douglas Martin, *The Baha'i Faith: The Emerging Global Religion.* India: Baha'i Publishing, 2003.
• J. E. Esslemont, *Baha'u'llah and the New Era: An Introduction to the Baha'i Faith.* India: Baha'i Publishing, 1980.

CHAPTER 7
PUTTING IT ALL TOGETHER

Thinking It Through

Focus: This session compares religious beliefs and suggests ways of approaching world religions from a Christian point of view.

In the first chapter, I introduced some imaginary churchgoers and their responses to world religions.

Rodney: I appreciate the approach that religions have toward life. You must respond to the world with the highest ideals of love and service. Even though religions teach different things, their core beliefs are very openhearted and positive—calling for a change of your heart toward God and other people. They call people to sincere discipline and high standards. That's why I have a *very* hard time with people who say that other religions hand you a phony bill of goods to get you off track. That's nonsense.

Becky: Yet why do we support preachers and missionaries if there isn't some reason why people should hear about Jesus? I'd love people to have a relationship with Christ as I do!

Gathering

Enjoy refreshments with other group members at the beginning of the session. Read Matthew 20:1-16, and remember that God is generous beyond human expectations of merit and fairness.

What was the best reward you ever received for doing something? What was the best gift you ever got? Think about rewards and gifts as you meditate on God's blessings.

Missionaries

Do you or your church support missionaries? Where are they located? What are the primary religions in the areas where they serve? After reading this study, are you more or less interested in supporting missionary outreach?

But at the same time I respect that people of other faiths are strong in their convictions, too. I wouldn't want someone of another faith to disrespect my beliefs, nor would I want them to bug me until I agreed with them. Instead, I'd like reciprocal love and respect to exist between that person and me.

Ted: On the other hand, I think it's important not to take a "share cookies" approach to world religions. You know, a dilettante attitude like some people espouse: "We all worship God, we all follow different paths, but all paths lead to God, so we should just celebrate our common traits, minimize the differences, and share our cookies instead of fighting." That, too, is fundamentally disrespectful of people's deepest beliefs.

Read over the section "Thinking It Through." Assume the roles of the characters in the conversation. Read the section aloud. Ad-lib your own responses. Which character best expresses your point of view? Explain.

Anisa: Although at this point I understand world religions a lot better, I still struggle as to how to put all these ideas together.

Basic Beliefs

Let us summarize what we have covered in this study. Recall the questions that I introduced in Chapter 1:

- What is the nature of God/divinity?
- What is sin?
- What is forgiveness, and on what basis is it conferred?
- What are the elements of worship?
- What are the ethical demands?
- What is the future beyond death?
- What is the view of other faiths?
- What are the scriptures?
- What are a few, quick historical highlights?

How would you answer these same questions concerning your Christian faith? Let me "walk through" several Christian beliefs and make some very basic comparisons between Christianity and other faiths. A quick overview like this misses many nuances and interrelated beliefs. Think about comparisons you would make and nuances you would introduce.

> Make a list of what you have learned about the different world religions. Use your list to make comparisons of your own between Christianity and these world religions.

Nature of God

The nature of God, especially the incarnation of God in Jesus Christ, stands at the center of Christian faith. Christians believe in the Lord God of the Jewish tradition and additionally affirm that God took bodily, human existence as a particular Jew: Jesus. He is the Messiah and God's Son. Christians affirm that the one God is known in three ways: Father, Son, and Holy Spirit. God's nature is to be "triune," yet one God.

> **God's Oneness**
> Why do you think it is important to affirm only one God? What would be the problem (hypothetically speaking) with more than one?
> How do you "conceptualize" the Trinity in your own mind and spirituality?

All the religions that we explored emphasize the one God, God's grace and goodness and righteousness, and God's worthiness to be worshiped. Jews and Muslims look to the one God, named YHWH and Allah in the respective traditions, who is the master and creator of the universe. Both faiths deny concepts that would compromise God's oneness, such as Trinity and Incarnation. Similarly, Sikhs believe in one God who creates and governs the cosmos, as does the Baha'i faith.

Hinduism affirms the one, changeless universal spirit, Brahman, although some Hindus worship varieties of incarnations of the universal spirit. Theravada Buddhism does not look to a supreme being and is not "theistic." Mahayana Buddhists look to the "Buddha nature," the eternal presence in the universe known through many enlightened beings called *bodhisattvas*.

Sin and Forgiveness

Christians understand sin as something deeper than bad moral choices. There is a flaw, "original sin," in human nature that makes impossible any pleasing God through positive actions. Jesus suffered, died on a cross, and rose from the dead in order to reveal God's intention toward us, which is reconciling love. God did for us what we cannot do for ourselves. Linking two Jewish ideas not previously conjoined, messiah and atonement, Christian belief in Jesus declares that through him God offers forgiveness, justification, sanctification, and eternal life. While salvation is not conferred because of our deeds, our deeds spring from our faith and love.

> **Original Sin**
> Do you find it easier to believe that human beings are both good and bad, or that humans are irrecoverably sinfully at the most basic level? If you affirm that God is merciful, is it necessary to affirm original sin? Why or why not?

Judaism, Islam, Baha'i, and Sikhism all affirm free will without original sin, and also the necessity of obedience in faith and love to God. All these faiths affirm the necessity and priority of God's grace and mercy. These faiths teach that human beings are prone to forget God and to put other things before God. Nevertheless human beings are trainable through religious discipline and obedience. Though God certainly reveals his will to human beings, an atoning sacrifice initiated on God's side is unnecessary.

Hinduism and Buddhism do not teach "sin" per se but karma, the spiritual and temporal consequences of our good and bad actions. Our true selves are not spiritually damaged souls but are aspects of the one universal spirit. Our souls are called "atman." Karma guides the quality of our ongoing cycles of rebirth. For some Hindus, we follow our dharma in order to please our deity. For other Hindus, we do good for its own sake. The results for our pilgrimage to moksha, though, are the same. Similarly Buddhists look to the liberation of our true selves from rebirth; and for that, the Four Noble Truths and Eightfold Path are sufficient. Sikhism also teaches renunciation of the ego through devotion to God.

Ethical Demands

Christian ethical demands include deeds and actions that spring from the "fruit of the Spirit," that is, the activity of the Holy Spirit in our lives that matures us in the spiritual attitudes like love, mercy, compassion, and justice. The teachings of the Jewish Scriptures, as well as those of Jesus and the New Testament writers, provide laws and principles.

The other faiths we have examined have codes of conduct as well, all centered upon worship, prayer, principles and laws for living, and laws for the proper treatment of other people, including, in some cases, laws for society as well as treatment of animals. Ethical demands are not simply general moral principles but have a dual direction: pleasing God and serving others. In Hinduism, ethical demands correspond to one's worship and one's dharma, aiming at moksha. Buddhism similarly teaches a set of principles that aim at liberation (nirvana) as well as personal and social transformation. Likewise, Sikhism teaches service to others, honest work, and devotion to God; and Baha'i principles include care for others, equality, and education. Judaism, Sikhism, and Baha'i are not ascetic religions, while devotion to God through asceticism is a possible route for devotees in Christianity, Islam, Hinduism, and Buddhism.

Worship

Christian worship includes sacraments and other means through which God's grace comes to us. Similarly, worship practices vary within world faiths. World faiths consider regular, and indeed daily acts of worship crucial in maintaining one's relationship with the divine and in transforming oneself spiritually. Jews worship in synagogues, Muslims in mosques, Hindus in temples, Sikhs in gurdwaras, and Baha'is in people's homes or in special worship houses. Baha'is, Jews, Muslims, and Sikhs have religious leaders but no priests, while some Hindu groups have priests and some Buddhist groups have monks. Buddhist worship stresses meditation toward enlightenment rather than adoration of God. Many kinds of Hinduism also stress meditation.

Future Beyond Death

Christians believe in a life beyond death and paradise for the righteous. Life beyond death may also mean eternal punishment. Some Christians believe in an intermediate state, Purgatory, wherein one is "purged" of sin's consequences in order eventually to reach heaven. Belief in Jesus as God's Son is the basic entry-point to eternal life.

Since the Tanakh deals very little with the afterlife, Jews disagree whether or not there is an afterlife and prefer to emphasize good works in this life. The Qur'an teaches fairly explicitly what heaven and hell are like: the torments of hell as well as the lushness and beauty of heaven.

Some kinds of Buddhism portray an afterlife of blessed reward, while others stress the joy of nirvana and the extinction of our selfish natures.

In Hinduism, "heaven" is moksha, or release from cycles of rebirth; and while "hell" is not exactly samsara (rebirth), one does seek release from the world. Neither Hinduism nor Buddhism would consider individual existence beyond death a suitable goal; rather, one seeks the extinction of the self, or the return of the soul to God. Baha'is consider heaven and hell as states of the soul rather than literal places, while Sikhism believes in karma, rebirth, and liberation similar to Hinduism.

View of Other Faiths

Many Christians say that, since belief in Jesus Christ is so crucial, then all who do not believe in him are lost. Why else go to all the trouble of having missionaries and preachers and evangelistic witnesses? Other Christians believe that God's grace is available to everyone. God will judge fairly those who never heard of Christ or who had sincere reasons not to believe in Jesus.

Jews believe they have no "corner" on religious truth. Baha'is believe that other religions are legitimate paths to God. Sikhs, too, believe that other paths lead to God, and their own path can be a way to help you in your own chosen path. Islam affirms that Jews and Christians are recipients of God's love and mercy, because they are monotheistic. Islam affirms no other faiths, however. Muslims consider Baha'i a heresy in part because Baha'i does recognize other religions as legitimate paths to God.

Hinduism, too, affirms many paths to God, as do most Buddhists. The meditation techniques can be practiced without embracing the beliefs of the religion.

> Log onto *amazon.com* or *barnesandnoble.com*. If you type in the key word *religion*, how many book titles will appear? Similarly, type in the key word *spirituality*. Take some time to look through these titles, noting authors, subjects of interest, and so on. Then type in the name of a particular religion. Make a "to read" list of books that you would like eventually to read.

Scriptures

Christian Scriptures include the Hebrew Bible, which Christians refer to as the Old Testament. The Scriptures also include the New Testament, which contains material concerning Jesus and the early church's beliefs and convictions about him. The New Testament is the same for all Christians, although the Old Testament in Roman Catholic and Orthodox canon includes some additional material called the Apocrypha.

Scriptures vary among world faiths. The Jewish Scripture is the Tanakh, the same books as the Old Testament but with a different ordering and tradition of translation. The Muslim scripture is the Holy Qur'an. The Sikh scripture is called the *Guru Granth Sahib*. The writings of the Bab and Baha'u'llah compose the sacred writings of Baha'i, while the sayings of Siddhartha as well as other "sutras" compose the scriptures of Buddhism. Hindus have a number of sacred writings, the most sacred of which are the *Vedas*.

History

It would be difficult to compare the histories of each religion, arising as they have during different times and different cultures. All religions, however, have changed and developed over the historical process. Christian history is of course very complex. Two major branches of Christianity, the Orthodox and the Roman Catholic, split in A.D. 1054, with both branches claiming historical continuity with the New Testament church. Beginning with Martin Luther's "reformation" of the early sixteenth century, Protestant churches have sprung from many historic sources, situations, and locations.

Ways to Consider

Our world is fairly bulging with religious variety and diversity. A recent article in *The Atlantic Monthly* by Toby Lester (February 2002) called attention to the fact that many brand new religions are developing in different parts of the world. Most people are ignorant of the religious variety in the world today.

We live in a pluralistic nation, which means that people of many different faiths live together in our society. Assuming that religious people

Find a copy in your local library of the February 2002 issue of *The Atlantic Monthly* containing Toby Lester's article, "Oh, Gods!" Or find the article at the magazine's Web site, *www.theatlantic.com*. Study the article. What are some of the issues Lester raises concerning twenty-first-century religions? What does the future look like for Christianity?

do not begin cloistering themselves into numerous mini-societies, how do we approach other religions from a Christian point of view? The introduction to this study considered several options. Let me build upon those ideas to conclude our study.

The way of *exclusivism* upholds one particular religion as the true one, while other religions are false. This way has obvious benefits if a person is a member of a particular religion because it honors the truth claims of the religion in question. Exclusivism, though, neglects the fact that world religions share so many common beliefs and principles. Exclusivism can lead to an unintentional religious arrogance. An exclusivist might consign to hell everyone who does not believe as he or she believes.

The way of *inclusivism* denies a single way to God, upholding the possibility of many different paths to God. No one religion can claim all truth and legitimacy. But this path overlooks the truth claims specific to particular religions. Inclusivism can also lead to an unintentional *reverse* religious arrogance, that is, labeling as "close minded" and "conservative" anyone who has taken a stand with a particular faith.

In his classic book *The World's Religions,* Huston Smith "likens [religions] to a stained glass window whose sections divide the light of the sun into different colors."[1] The light is God; the sections and colors are different religions. This way shifts the emphasis from the truth of particular religions to ultimate reality itself. To accept this way, one would have to affirm that God's truth is only partially expressed in religious beliefs. Some religious people would agree; our religious language is symbolic and only approximates the fullness of God's

Check the Web site for the Harvard Pluralism Project, *www.pluralism.org*. Also check out the Religious Movements Homepage at The University of Virginia, *www.religiousmovements.org*

See also the Pluralism Project's CD-ROM, *On Common Ground: World Religions in America,* published by Columbia University Press.

glory. Others would say God's truth is very adequately expressed in religious dogmas and beliefs, albeit in human language.

A slightly different way is to say: All religions are trying to reach the same goal, but by different ways. One temptation of this view, as James C. Livingston suggests, is that, as one delves deeper into religious beliefs, one's own religion still

> Several notable authors in academia have discussed issues about pluralism and world religions: for instance John Hick, Ninian Smart, John Cobb, Schubert Ogden, and others. Dig a little deeper into these issues by reading some of their books, available on line or through your local library.

dominates as the highest form of religion![2] In other words, if Hindu thinkers say, "all religions aim at the same goal," the stated religious goals will sound Hindu. This way does, however, respect the sincerity and discipline of persons who have devoted their lives to religions other than one's own.

Some authors have suggested another way: Jesus is *the* way to God, *but* he speaks in different ways *through* other religions, albeit in unrecognized ways.[3] For instance, if you think back to John 14:6b ("No one comes to the Father except through me"), you would interpret that verse to mean, *Jesus himself*, rather than only *belief in* Jesus, is the way to God. *Jesus himself* makes himself known in different religious symbols and cultures. One problem with this view, however, is that it makes all religious people "really" Christian. As a Christian would not be considered "really" a Hindu, for instance, a person of another faith would not want "really" to be Christian.

Another way, developed by S. Mark Heim, is to concentrate upon the truth of religious *goals*. For instance, if you are a Buddhist, you really can reach a state of nirvana, which is freedom from desire and attachment. If you are a Jew, you really can bear witness to God by practicing righteousness. If you are a Christian, you really can find justification and eternal life in Christ. You do not have to fret about which religion is true, because we will always disagree about that. But you can say, all religions are "real" and all religions offer some attractive goals for people.[4]

The problem is, some religious goals are contradictory. Nevertheless, this way does affirm many of the "results" that religious people have truly achieved over the centuries. This way also affirms the fact that religions can strengthen one another through shared practices.

Christian Convictions

Now that we have surveyed these faiths, let us ask: Does an uncompromising faith necessarily mean rejection of other faiths? Or can you be strong in your Christian beliefs while respecting other faiths? My own answer to these questions are No and Yes, respectively.

I began this study with some classic Christian texts that justify the need for evangelistic outreach. One is Acts 4:12 ("There is salvation in no one else, for there is no other name under heaven . . . by which we must be saved"). Another is John 14:6b ("No one comes to the Father except through me"). These Scriptures, and others, make pretty clear how one receives God's free gifts. For many Christians, the case is thus closed. Jesus called people to take a stand, to leave their homes and their wealth in order to follow him. In Chapter 1, I suggested that additional Scriptures take the discussion to a different place: Matthew 7:21-23; Matthew 25:31-46; and others. These Scriptures do not

> Reread the Scriptures discussed here, in addition to some of the Scriptures discussed in Chapter 1. In what ways, if any, has your thinking changed concerning these issues? Explain.

"replace" the more exclusive Acts 4:12 and John 14:6b, nor do the Acts and John passages "replace" the verses from Matthew. To cite another example, Romans 1:19-21 also implies, although in harsh language, that God's will has been made known in ways apart from Hebrew history. But if we are true to all the Scriptures, if we do not turn particular verses into discussion-ending slogans, we can find grounds to respect and honor the beliefs of others.

When Jesus told his disciples, "No one comes to the Father except through me," was he talking about Hindus and Buddhists and Zoroastrians and Taoists and what would happen to them in the afterlife? Was he talking about Christianity as a world religion? Following a recent commentator, I believe he was reassuring his friends, since he was shortly to die, that he, Jesus, would never, ever leave them, nor would God the Father.[5] When the disciples themselves faced death, they remembered his assurance. They also remembered his commandment, which was to love one another.

If you approach world faiths with love, you can have convictions about your own faith and also you can respect other people's faith and love them "as yourself."[6] You can be secure in your own religious traditions; but you can also be humble rather than haughty when you meet someone who does not believe the same as you. Paul said that we can be truly impressive in our religious beliefs and our religious "results," but without love, we gain nothing (1 Corinthians 13:1-3). People who love one another respect one another and truly listen to one another.

"O the depth of the riches and wisdom and knowledge of God! How unsearchable are his judgments and how inscrutable his ways! . . . For from him and through him and to him are all things. To him be the glory forever. Amen" (Romans 11:33, 36).

> **Closing**
>
> Light a candle and think about some of the goals of these religions:
>
> • Love
> • Knowing God
> • Inner peace
> • Service to others
> • Peace among peoples
> • Spiritual freedom
> • Reconciliation with others
> • Witness to truth
>
> Conclude by reading together 1 Corinthians 13.

Notes

1. Huston Smith, *The World's Religions: Our Great Wisdom Traditions* (San Francisco: HarperSanFrancisco, 1991), page 386.

2. James C. Livingston, *Anatomy of the Sacred: An Introduction to Religion* (Upper Saddle River, NJ: Prentice Hall, 1998), pages 422–26.

3. See, for instance, James L. Fredericks, *Faith among Faiths: Christian Theology and Non-Christian Religions*, Paulist Press, 1999.

4. S. Mark Heim, *The Depth of the Riches: A Trinitarian Theology of Religious Ends,* Grand Rapids: Eerdmans, 2000.

5. See Gail R. O'Day, "The Gospel of John," in *The New Interpreter's Bible* (Nashville: Abingdon Press, 1995), vol. 9, pages 743–45.

6. See Theodore Runyon, *The New Creation: John Wesley's Theology Today* (Nashville: Abingdon Press, 1998), pages 200–21, wherein Runyon discusses Wesley's belief that conviction and tolerance both spring from God's love in our hearts.